THE OPEN SECRET

The Open Secret

n/ot

Hannah Whitall Smith
Abridged and Adapted by Ann Spangler

SERVANT BOOKS
Ann Arbor, Michigan

Published by Servant Books
P.O. Box 8617
Ann Arbor, Michigan 48107

Cover Photo by Russ Lamb, H. Armstrong Roberts
Book Design by John B. Leidy

Scripture taken from the HOLY BIBLE; NEW INTERNA-
TIONAL VERSION copyright © 1978 by the International
Bible Society. Used by permission of Zondervan Bible Pub-
lishers.

Printed in the United States of America
ISBN 0-89283-195-2

Library of Congress Cataloging in Publication Data

Smith, Hannah Whitall, 1832-1911.
  The Open Secret.

  1. Christian life.   I. Spangler, Ann.   II. Title.
BV4501.S665 1984   248.4   84-10511
ISBN 0-89283-195-2 (pbk.)

Contents

Foreword

HANNAH WHITALL SMITH has captivated millions of people with the message of *The Christian's Secret of a Happy Life*. Her writings speak graciously of the love of God, of his forgiveness, his patience, and his call to men and women to know him personally. Reared in a Quaker family, Hannah Smith believed firmly that the Bible revealed its secrets only to those who read it with patience, faith, and the willingness to obey its precepts. Hence, the title of this work, *The Open Secret*.

Whoever wants to uncover the secret, must come to the Bible with a believing heart. No amount of intellectual curiosity will substitute for faith. For the new Christian, Hannah Smith offers wise guidance along the path of the Christian life. For the seasoned believer, she provides words of encouragement and exhortation, a call to become more like Christ himself.

It is clear that Hannah Smith practiced what she preached. She read the scriptures eagerly, making rich personal application of whatever she read. The fruits of her own careful reading and study are evident in the pages that follow. Though she wrote a century ago, her writing is yet fresh and her insights compelling. To take full advantage of these insights, the reader will do well to savor *The Open Secret*, to read it slowly, and to ponder it carefully in the presence of God.

Each chapter of *The Open Secret* contains the core of a Bible study on a particular theme of scripture. As such, it can be used as a springboard for further study as well as for meditation.

This edition has been abridged and adapted for modern readers. The original work contained a few chapters that were written as outlines, rather than full descriptions of the themes covered. These have been omitted in order to present a more unified and readable book. The original also contained many more scripture quotations. Those that were not as central to the text are simply listed in parentheses after the quotations that were retained. The reader who is interested in a full treatment of the subject will want to consult these passages in order to consider them more carefully.

The New International Version of the Bible has been substituted for the King James Version, except in places where the King James seemed intricately connected to the point Hannah Smith was making. Occasionally, it was necessary to rewrite phrases or to delete examples that would sound particularly quaint to modern ears. In most cases the author's words have not been changed.

Where I have taken liberties with the text, my intention has been to communicate more effectively to the modern reader. Where I have failed in this effort, I beg the author's pardon, confident that she would grant it were she here to do so.

ANN SPANGLER

Introduction

How to Prepare Bible Lessons

For your study of the Bible you require four things:

1. A Bible with references, if possible.
2. A complete Cruden's, or Young's "Analytical Concordance."
3. A blank-book that can be ruled in columns.
4. An undisturbed desk or table, where you can keep the above three things with pen and ink always ready.

Having provided these few necessary things, proceed as follows:

1. Commit yourself, in a few words, to the Lord, asking for light and guidance, and expecting to receive them.
2. Choose a subject appropriate to the occasion.
3. Find in the concordance all the words referring to this subject, and select from among the texts given, such as seem to you best to elucidate it, noting them down under their appropriate headings in your blank-book.
4. Read over these selected texts carefully, and make a list of the most striking on a separate piece of paper, putting them in the order that will best develop the lesson. Begin this list with a familiar text, and gradually progress to those not so well known, letting each successive text develop the subject a little more clearly than the last. Close the list, if possible, with some practical instance from Bible history, or some typical illustration.
5. Having thus prepared your list, open your Bible at the first text, and on the margin beside it write the reference to the second text on your list. Turn to this second one, and write

beside it the reference to the third. Turn to the third, and write beside it the reference to the fourth. And so on through the whole list. Finally, refer back to your foundation text, and sum the subject all up.

6. On a blank page at the end of your Bible, write down an index of all the subjects you have thus studied, with a reference at each to the first text on your list concerning that subject. If you have no blank leaves at the end of your Bible, gum the edge of a half sheet of note paper and fasten it in.

7. If you prefer it, you may write a list of all your chain of texts on the margin beside the first text, so as to have them all before you at once to choose from.

8. By this plan you will have a complete chain of texts on any given subject running all through your Bible itself, each verse referring you to the next one you wish to read, without having the trouble of loose slips of paper to embarrass you. Also, having once studied out a subject, you have it all ready for any future use; and by turning to your index list, you can at a moment's notice open your Bible at the foundation text, and can then turn to one text after another through the whole course of your lesson, without hesitation or embarrassment.

HANNAH WHITALL SMITH
Germantown, Pennsylvania

ONE

The Assurance of Faith

Foundation Text— *Let us draw near to God with a sincere heart in full assurance of faith, having our hearts sprinkled to cleanse us from a guilty conscience and having our bodies washed with pure water.* —Heb 10:22

By the assurance of faith is meant a clear and definite knowledge of the forgiveness of sins, of reconciliation with God, and of our relationship with him as our Father.

About these vital matters we must be able to say, "I know." Not "I hope so," or "I wish so," but firmly and unhesitatingly, "I know."

Blessed are those who have learned to acclaim you, / who walk in the light of your presence, O Lord. / They rejoice in your name all day long; / they exult in your righteousness.—Ps 89:15-16

Then you will know that I, the Lord, am your Savior, your Redeemer, the Mighty One of Jacob.—Is 60:16

On that day you will realize that I am in my Father, and you are in me, and I am in you.—Jn 14:20

This assurance is necessary for all right living. It ought to be the first step in the Christian life. In the absence of this assurance, lies the secret of much of the failure of Christians. They present the strange anomaly of children who doubt their parentage, of heirs who are afraid to take possession of their inheritance, of a bride who is not sure she has been really married.

What could we expect from such doubts in earthly relationships, but indifference, fear, anxiety, unkindness, sorrow, and rebellion?

And are not these the very things that are found far too often in the hearts of God's children, in reference to their relationships to him?

> Because you did not serve the Lord your God joyfully and gladly in the time of prosperity, therefore in hunger and thirst, in nakedness and dire poverty, you will serve the enemies the Lord sends against you. he will put an iron yoke on your neck until he has destroyed you.—Dt 28:47-48

No soul can serve the Lord with joyfulness who is in doubt as to the reality or the stability of its relations with him. All human comfort is destroyed in such a case, as affecting earthly relations; and but little divine comfort is, as we all know, to be found in doubtful spiritual relations.

Can we then suppose for a moment that this too frequent reign of doubt in Christians' hearts was God's plan for his people? Does the Bible teach that it is?

I answer most emphatically, No, a thousand times No!

The Old Testament never contemplated the idea of Israelites, who did not know whether they were Israelites or not. Every law given to them or promise made, was founded on the previously acknowledged and understood fact, that they did in very truth belong to the family of Israel, and were indeed the people of God.

Before they were allowed to join the Lord's army and fight his battles, they had to "indicate their ancestry."

> "Take a census of the whole Israelite community by their clans and families, listing every man by name, one by one. You and Aaron are to number by their divisions all the men in Israel twenty years

old or more who are able to serve in the army. One man from each tribe, each the head of his family, is to help you. . . . and they called the whole community together on the first day of the second month. The people indicated their ancestry by their clans and families, and the men twenty years old or more were listed by name, one by one.—Nm 1:2-4, 18

And before they could enter into the office of priest they must "search for their family records"; for no strangers were allowed to "approach the sanctuary."

Appoint Aaron and his sons to serve as priests; anyone else who approaches the sanctuary must be put to death.—Nm 3:10

These searched for their family records, but they could not find them and so were excluded from the priesthood as unclean. The governor ordered them not to eat any of the most sacred food until there was a priest ministering with the Urim and Thummim.—Ezr 2:62-63

And similarly we, who are God's people now, cannot effectively fight his battles nor enjoy true priestly communion with him, until we also can "indicate our ancestry," know that we *are* the children of God, and that we are born of him.

Because you are sons, God sent the Spirit of his Son into our hearts, the Spirit who calls out, "*Abba,* Father." So you are no longer a slave, but a son; and since you are a son, God has made you also an heir.—Gal 4:6-7 (Jn 3:1-2)

We cannot have the spirit of a son, until we know we are sons. To doubt it, would be to lose the spirit at once.

Those who are led by the Spirit of God are sons of God. For you did not receive a spirit that makes you a slave again to fear, but you received the Spirit of sonship. And by him we cry, "*Abba,* Father." The Spirit himself testifies with our spirit that we are God's children. Now if we are children, then we are heirs—heirs of God and coheirs with Christ, if indeed we share in his sufferings in order that we may also share in his glory.—Rom 8:14-17

Our Lord himself always speaks to his disciples in terms of absolute certainty as to their relations to God.

> I have given them the glory that you gave me, that they may be one as we are one: I in them and you in me. May they be brought to complete unity to let the world know that you sent me and have loved them even as you have loved me. —Jn 17:22-23

> "Do not let your hearts be troubled. Trust in God; trust also in me. In my Father's house are many rooms; if it were not so, I would have told you. I am going there to prepare a place for you. And if I go and prepare a place for you, I will come back and take you to be with me that you also may be where I am."
> —Jn 14:1-3 (Lk 10:20; 12:32)

"If it were not so he would have told us." Surely we may trust him, and accept his statements as facts, without any further questioning.

Nowhere in Acts do we find the apostles or any of the early believers, questioning their standing, or doubting their relationship to the Lord. Peter said concerning their experiences on the day of Pentecost:

> This is what was spoken by the prophet Joel: "In the last days, God says, I will pour out my Spirit on all people. Your sons and daughters will prophesy, your young men will see visions, your old men will dream dreams. Even on my servants, both men and women, I will pour out my Spirit in those days, and they will prophesy."—Acts 2:16-18 (Acts 4:9-10, 20)

No one can read the history of the words and deeds of the apostles and the early believers, without seeing that they were saturated through and through with an utter certainty of their salvation in the Lord Jesus Christ. It was as much a part of them, as their nationality as Jews, or their nativity in Israel, and was no more open to question. Let us try to imagine them as being filled with the doubtings and questionings of modern Christians, and think what effect it would have had upon their preaching and their work. We can see in a moment that it would have been fatal to the spread of the gospel, and that a Church founded on doubts and questionings, could have made no headway in an unbelieving world.

This tone of utter assurance runs through all the Epistles. They are every one addressed to people of whom it was taken for granted that they knew their standing as the reconciled and forgiven children of God; and the writers express the same assurance for themselves, as they do for those to whom they write.

> Paul, Silas, and Timothy, to the church of the Thessalonians in God the Father and the Lord Jesus Christ:
> Grace and peace to you.
> We always thank God for all of you, mentioning you in our prayers. We continually remember before our God and Father your work produced by faith, your labor prompted by love, and your endurance inspired by hope in our Lord Jesus Christ.
> Brothers loved by God, we know that he has chosen you.
> —1 Thes 1:1-4

Again, if we run through the Epistles we shall invariably find that they also, like the Gospels and the Acts, are saturated through and through with assurance. Nowhere is a doubt or a question of the believer's standing in the family of God even so much as hinted at or supposed possible.

> Who shall separate us from the love of Christ? Shall trouble or hardship or persecution or famine or nakedness or danger or sword? As it is written: "For your sake we face death all day long; we are considered as sheep to be slaughtered." No, in all these things we are more than conquerors through him who loved us. For I am convinced that neither death nor life, neither angels nor demons, neither the present nor the future, nor any powers, neither height nor depth, nor anything else in all creation, will be able to separate us from the love of God that is in Christ Jesus our Lord.—Rom 8:35-39

> Praise be to the God and Father of our Lord Jesus Christ, who has blessed us in the heavenly realms with every spiritual blessing in

Christ. For he chose us in him before the creation of the world to be holy and blameless in his sight. In love he predestined us to be adopted as his sons through Jesus Christ, in accordance with his pleasure and will—to the praise of his glorious grace, which he has freely given us in the One he loves. In him we have redemption through his blood, the forgiveness of sins, in accordance with the riches of God's grace that he lavished on us with all wisdom and understanding.—Eph 1:3-8 (Eph 2:13; 1 Pt 1:3-5; Rom 5:1-2; 1 Cor 3:16-17; 1 Cor 6:19-20; Gal 3:26-27; Eph 1:3-8, 2:13; Col 1:12-14; Col 2:13-14; 1 Jn 2:12-14; 1 Pt 2:9)

These are only a few samples of the voice of every Epistle. Notice the assured expressions " *has* blessed," "*has* chosen," "we have redemption." Notice also the present tense of possession continually used, "are," "have," "has," "is." Never once is there a "hope so," or "perhaps so," or "I wish it might be so." Unquestioning, rejoicing assurance breathes from every word.

All exhortations to holiness are based on this assured knowledge of our reconciliation with God; and all exhortations to service also.

Since we have these promises, dear friends, let us purify ourselves from everything that contaminates body and spirit, perfecting holiness out of reverence for God.—2 Cor 7:1

We are not to be holy in order to gain the promises, but because we *have* the promises.

Set your minds on things above, not on earthly things. For you died, and your life is now hidden with Christ in God. When Christ, who is your life, appears, then you also will appear with him in glory.
    Put to death, therefore, whatever belongs to your earthly nature: sexual immorality, impurity, lust, evil desires and greed, which is idolatry.—Col 3:2-5 (Eph 4:30-32; 1 Jn 3:1-3)

God wants from us the service of a *son*, not of a *servant* only. A servant works for wages, a son from love. The servant works to gain something; the son because all has been given him. How can we render the son's service, unless we know that we *are* sons?

> So you are no longer a slave, but a son; and since you are a son, God has made you also an heir.—Gal 4:7 (Eph 5:1-2)

Since then we have proved thus incontrovertibly that the assurance of faith is the only normal condition of a child of God, our next point must be as to how it is to be arrived at.

We answer that it comes simply by *believing God*. He says certain things about himself and about us; faith believes them, and assurance follows. Notice that in the scriptures "believing" and "having" are always joined together. "He that believes, has," is the continual declaration!

> I tell you the truth, he who believes has everlasting life.—Jn 6:47

> Just as Moses lifted up the snake in the desert, so the Son of Man must be lifted up, that everyone who believes in him may have eternal life.
>
> For God so loved the world that he gave his one and only Son, that whoever believes in him shall not perish but have eternal life. For God did not send his Son into the world to condemn the world, but to save the world through him. Whoever believes in him is not condemned, but whoever does not believe stands condemned already because he has not believed in the name of God's one and only Son.—Jn 3:14-18

> Then Jesus declared, "I am the bread of life. He who comes to me will never go hungry, and he who believes in me will never be thirsty."—Jn 6:35 (Jn 1:12; 3:36; 5:24; 11:25-26; 20:30-31)

Notice that it never says, "he that feels, has" but always "he who believes." Our feelings are no guide whatever here. In all matters of fact, it is folly to depend upon feelings; and, in truth, we never do it in our earthly affairs. We never say over a piece of good or bad news, "Do I *feel* it is true," but we confine ourselves simply to the question, " *Is* it true?"

Who would be so silly as to enter a railroad depot and take

the first train at hand, and then sit down and try to "feel" whether it was the right train or not? We all know that the state of our feelings could not alter the facts; and our sole aim in such cases is always to find out the facts.

In order for assurance of faith then, as to our relations with the Lord, we must not depend upon our feelings, but must simply find out the facts.

God's order, and the order of good common sense as well, is always *1. Fact, 2. Faith, 3. Feeling.* But in matters of religion man reverses this order, and says *1. Feeling, 2. Faith, 3. Fact.*

And just as in the case of the railway train we would find peace and assurance by asking some one who knew, and by believing his word, so also in the case of our relations with the Lord, we must hear and believe what he says about it, without regard to how we feel.

> We accept man's testimony, but God's testimony is greater because it is the testimony of God, which he has given about his Son. Anyone who believes in the Son of God has this testimony in his heart. Anyone who does not believe God has made him out to be a liar, because he has not believed the testimony God has given about his Son. And this is the testimony: God has given us eternal life, and this life is in his Son.—Jn 5:9-11

We receive "man's testimony" continually without a question or doubt; shall we be less ready to receive "God's testimony?" In verse ten notice that it is not he who has this testimony in his heart who shall believe, but he who believes shall have this testimony in his heart.

Here we have, first the fact, second the faith, third the feeling.

What are we to do then in order to get the assurance of faith?

> Then they asked him, "What must we do to do the works God requires?"
> Jesus answered, "The work of God is this: to believe in the one he has sent."—Jn 6:28-29

We must believe two things. First, what God says concerning Christ. Second, what he says concerning us.

It is not really believing a person if we only believe half he says; and yet many who would consider it the worst of sins to disbelieve God's testimony concerning Christ, consider it no sin at all, but in fact rather virtuous humility, to doubt his testimony concerning themselves. They dare not doubt that Jesus is the Christ, but find no difficulty in doubting whether they are themselves "born of God." And yet God joins the two inseparably together.

> Everyone who believes that Jesus is the Christ is born of God, and everyone who loves the father loves his child as well.—1 Jn 5:1

Here is a plain and simple statement. "Everyone who believes, *is* born," not will be, but is, now in the present moment; for no one can believe who is not born of God.

But you may say, how can I know that I believe? Could you write a paper saying, "I do not believe that Jesus is the Christ" and sign it with your name? Would it not be a lie if you should do so? If the alternative were presented to you of denying Christ or going to prison, would you not choose the prison?

You do believe, therefore, that Jesus is the Christ; and God says that whosoever does, *is* born of him. Does not this settle the question?

> If anyone acknowledges that Jesus is the Son of God, God lives in him and he in God.—1 Jn 4:15

Could language be plainer than this? If you confess that Jesus is the Son of God, God dwells in you, now.

> But what does it say? "The word is near you; it is in your mouth and in your heart," that is, the word of faith we are proclaiming: That if you confess with your mouth, "Jesus is Lord," and believe in your heart that God raised him from the dead, you will be saved.—Rom 10:8-9

What should we think of a child who should doubt whether she was really her mother's own child; who should say, "Well, I have a trembling hope I am, but that is all?" Would not such expressions be equivalent to casting a doubt on the mother's word? And do not our doubts as to whether we are really God's children " make him a liar?"

> Anyone who believes in the Son of God has this testimony in his heart. Anyone who does not believe God has made him out to be a liar, because he has not believed the testimony God has given about his Son. And this is the testimony: God has given us eternal life, and this life is in his Son.—1 Jn 5:10-11

The testimony we are to believe is that "God has given us eternal life." If he has given it, we must have it, and there is nothing more to be said about it.

> I write these things to you who believe in the name of the Son of God so that you may know that you have eternal life.—1 Jn 5:13

We *have* eternal life if we believe; but we may not "*know*" that we have it, and our peace depends upon our knowing it. A man may have a fortune left to him by a friend, but until he "knows it," he cannot enjoy it.

The assurance of faith, therefore, is simply the "knowing" of which John speaks. And it arises from our belief in the trustworthy testimony, not of our feelings, but of God's word.

> Jesus did many other miraculous signs in the presence of his disciples, which are not recorded in this book. But these are written that you may believe that Jesus is the Christ, the Son of God, and that by believing you may have life in his name.
> —Jn 20:30-31

Not what we feel, but what is on the record; not what are our experiences, but what has been "written"; this is the foundation for the assurance of faith.

We all of us know the curious experience of being "turned round" when walking in the streets of a city or traveling in a railroad car, when we feel as if we were going in one direction, although as a fact we are going in exactly the opposite direction. Our feelings in this case contradict the facts, and we may even know this; and yet it is almost impossible not to yield to these feelings and take the wrong direction. I have discovered that I can conquer these feelings, and turn myself round right, by just repeating over to myself in a very emphatic way, when I *feel* that I am going north yet know as a fact that I am going south, "I am, I *am*, I am going south." In a minute or two my feelings always come under the control of the fact, and I begin to feel, as well as to know, that I really am going south.

In the same way, when we have convinced ourselves from God's "record" that our sins are forgiven and that our peace is made with God, we can then control our feeling that it is not so, by a similar process. We can assert on the authority of God's word, "My sins *are* forgiven; I *am* God's child; God *is* reconciled to me; I *am* a Christian."

Such a course, persevered in regardless of feeling, will always bring peace and deliverance to every soul that is willing to take God at his word, and to risk all on his trustworthiness.

TWO

God Keeps Us Safe

Foundation Text— *"I am with you and will watch over you wherever you go, and I will bring you back to this land. I will not leave you until I have done what I have promised you."*
—Gn 28:15 (RSV)

We all feel the need of being *kept* by a power outside of ourselves. Life is full of dangers to both soul and body, and we are most of the time too blind to see them. We are like little helpless, ignorant children, walking in strange pathways, and knowing nothing of the snares and pitfalls that await our unwary steps.

We have need to cry out continually with the Psalmist:

But my eyes are fixed on you, O Sovereign Lord; / in you I take refuge—do not give me over to death. / Keep me from the snares they have laid for me, / from the traps set by evildoers.
—Ps 141:8-9

And continually we have the Lord's answer:

For he will command his angels concerning you / to guard you in all your ways; / they will lift you up in their hands, / so that you will not strike your foot against a stone. / You will tread upon the lion and the cobra; / you will trample the great lion and the serpent.—Ps 91:11-13

15

Then you will go on your way in safety, / and your foot will not stumble; / when you lie down, you will not be afraid; / when you lie down, your sleep will be sweet. / Have no fear of sudden disaster / or of the ruin that overtakes the wicked, / for the Lord will be your confidence / and will keep your foot from being snared.—Prv 3:23-26

The Lord is like a mother who holds the hand of her little child as they walk together, that she may keep it from falling over the snares that lie in its way. It is the mother holding the child that makes it safe, not the child holding the mother. Notice the words "lift you up," illustrated by the infant in the mother's arms, safe because of her upholding. Its little frightened gasps when danger is near, do not make it any safer, for its safety consists in the fact that its mother holds it, and everything depends on whether *she* is able to keep it safe.

To him who is able to keep you from falling and to present you before his glorious presence without fault and with great joy.
—Jude 24

Mothers are not always able to keep their children from falling, but God is always able.

I, the Lord, watch over it; / I water it continually. / I guard it day and night / so that no one may harm it.—Is 27:3

Our hearts are like a garden open on every side to enemies who are pressing in to ravage and destroy; and there is no safety for us except in the keeping power of the Divine Husbandman, who neither slumbers nor sleeps, and whom no enemy can either elude or conquer.

"Hear the word of the Lord, O nations; / proclaim it in distant coastlands: / 'He who scattered Israel will gather them / and will watch over his flock like a shepherd.' "—Jer 31:10

We are like the poor helpless sheep who have no armor against their enemies, and no wisdom to save themselves from danger. But we have a Divine Shepherd to care for us, and therefore we need not fear.

> For the Lord's portion is his people, / Jacob his allotted inheritance. / In a desert land he found him, / in a barren and howling waste. / He shielded him and cared for him; / he guarded him as the apple of his eye.—Dt 32:9-10

Nothing is dearer to a man or more tenderly cared for than the apple of his eye. And since we are to the Lord "as the apple of his eye," we must be sure of the tenderest divine keeping.

> Show the wonder of your great love, / you who save by your right hand / those who take refuge in you from their foes. / Keep me as the apple of your eye; / hide me in the shadow of your wings. / from the wicked who assail me, / from my mortal enemies who surround me.—Ps 17:7-9

The mother hen keeps her little chickens under the shadow of her wings, and so will the Lord keep us, *if* we will let him. But this is a very large "if." What would we think of a little chicken which should stand off by itself, trembling with fright when danger was near, and saying, "I am not worthy to go under my mother's wing. I am too little, and too weak, and too insignificant. I must wait to go under until I am stronger and more worthy of her love?" Would not the mother hen have answered such a foolish little chicken by saying, "It is just because you *are* little and weak that I am spreading out my wings to cover you, and am clucking for you to come. If you were grown large and strong I would not want you. Your littleness and your weakness are your claim to my care."

Is there nothing in this parable to teach us a lesson?

> He who dwells in the shelter of the Most High / will rest in the shadow of the Almighty. / I will say of the Lord, "he is my refuge and my fortress, / my God, in whom I trust." / Surely he will save you from the fowler's snare / and from the deadly pestilence. / He will cover you with his feathers, / and under his wings you will find refuge; / his faithfulness will be your shield and rampart. /

You will not fear the terror of night, / nor the arrow that flies by day. —Ps 91:1-5 (6-10)

Have we never said, or at least thought, that we were too weak and unworthy to make the Lord our refuge; and have we not sometimes in our secret hearts planned to seek this refuge when we should feel ourselves more worthy of entering it?

My help comes from the Lord, / the Maker of heaven and earth. / He will not let your foot slip— / he who watches over you will not slumber; / indeed, he who watches over Israel / will neither slumber nor sleep. / The Lord watches over you— / the Lord is your shade at your right hand; / the sun will not harm you by day, / nor the moon by night. / The Lord will keep you from all harm— / he will watch over your life; / the Lord will watch over your coming and going / both now and forevermore.

—Ps 121:2-8

This Psalm might be called the Bible Keep. The Keep in an ancient castle was always the strongest and best protected room in the Castle, the one which could be the last reached by any enemy. In this Keep all the sick and weak and helpless inmates of the Castle were hidden in every time of danger. The qualification for entrance was simply and only, need and weakness. How foolish then it would have been for any to have made their weakness the reason for remaining outside! And yet how continually is this done towards the Lord's Keep.

The Lord protects the simplehearted; / when I was in great need, he saved me. / Be at rest once more, O my soul, / for the Lord has been good to you. / For you, O Lord, have delivered my soul from death, / my eyes from tears, / my feet from stumbling.

—Ps 116:6-8

It is the simple, the weak, those who are "brought low" whom the Lord preserves.

Notice the fact that this Divine Keeper never slumbers nor sleeps, and therefore never neglects those for whom he cares. Think of the fatal consequences of neglect on the part of keepers of a prison, or keepers of a flock of sheep, or keepers of a vineyard on a frosty night, or sentinels keeping a dangerous outpost, and show by contrast what sort of a Keeper our Lord is.

We all realize the responsibilities of the human keeper to whose care anything has been committed. When anything is given to ourselves to keep, we feel that we must care for that thing in preference to our own, if there is any choice. And from these high ideals of responsibility in our own case we may learn what our Divine Keeper must necessarily do.

I will remain in the world no longer, but they are still in the world, and I am coming to you. Holy Father, protect them by the power of your name—the name you gave me—so that they may be one as we are one. While I was with them, I protected them and kept them safe by that name you gave me. None has been lost except the one doomed to destruction so that Scripture would be fulfilled.
—Jn 17:11-12

For I have come down from heaven not to do my will but to do the will of him who sent me. And this is the will of him who sent me, that I shall lose none of all that he has given me, but raise them up at the last day.—Jn 6:38-39

We may therefore commit ourselves with the utmost confidence to the keeping of the Lord our Keeper.

So then, those who suffer according to God's will should commit themselves to their faithful Creator and continue to do good.—1 Pt 4:19

For our Creator is our Keeper. And he is a *faithful* Creator. Men whom we trust often prove unfaithful, but he never! And if *we* are grieved when doubts are felt of our faithfulness to any trust committed to us, how much more must he.

This is what God the Lord says— / he who created the heavens and stretched them out, / who spread out the earth and all that comes out of it, / who gives breath to its people, / and life to those who walk on it: / "I, the Lord, have called you in

righteousness; / I will take hold of your hand. / I will keep you
and will make you / to be a covenant for the people / and a light
for the Gentiles—Is 42:5-6 (2 Thes 3:3)

Therefore Paul could say:

That is why I am suffering as I am. Yet I am not ashamed, because I
know whom I have believed, and am convinced that he is able to
guard what I have entrusted to him for that day.—2 Tm 1:12

If we know him, we can not fail to trust him. No one who
knows him ever did yet. And this after all is the true secret of
confidence—knowledge of the trustworthiness of the one to
be trusted. We act on this in our earthly affairs, and are never
so silly as to look inside ourselves to see whether we can or
ought to trust another. We look at that other instead, and try
to find out his character and his ways. But in their intercourse
with the Lord many act on an entirely different principle. They
look at themselves for a warrant and ground of trust, instead of
at him. They behold self and its untrustworthiness, and are
filled with doubts and despair. Whereas a single soul-look at
him will fill us with perfect peace, because of *his* utter
trustworthiness.

You will keep in perfect peace / him whose mind is steadfast, /
because he trusts in you.—Is 26:3

Emphasize the words "perfect peace," and illustrate them by
the peace that comes when we have entrusted any precious
thing to safe-keeping. A bank for instance. Think how we are
continually trusting banks, and how comfortable we feel when
we have transferred our money from our own keeping to that
of some safe bank. Illustrate what trust in God ought to be, by
the nature of our trust in the bank. Show the folly of doubt, by
the folly of every hour running back to the bank to see if our
money is safe. And, by the indignation of the bank officers at
such a course, show how our doubts and fears must grieve our
God.

Our part in this divine keeping is threefold, as it always is in every stage of the spiritual life. We must *yield,* and *trust* and *obey.*

How great is your goodness, / which you have stored up for those who fear you, / which you bestow in the sight of men / on those who take refuge in you. / In the shelter of your presence you hide them / from the intrigues of men; / in your dwelling you keep them safe / from the strife of tongues.—Ps 31:19-20 (Ps 25:20)

There can be no keeping without yielding and trusting. In the very nature of things, a keeper must have that which he is to keep, entrusted utterly to his care.

Neither can there be any keeping without obedience.

My son, keep your father's commands / and do not forsake your mother's teaching. / Bind them upon your heart forever; / fasten them around your neck. / When you walk, they will guide you; / when you sleep, they will watch over you; / when you awake, they will speak to you. / For these commands are a lamp, / this teaching is a light, / and the correction of discipline / are the way to life, / keeping you from the immoral woman, / from the smooth tongue of the wayward wife.
—Prv 6:20-24 (Prv 4:4-6; Dt 7:11-12)

If we would be kept, we must be guided, and must follow that guidance.

It was the Lord our God himself who brought us and our forefathers up out of Egypt, from that land of slavery, and performed those great signs before our eyes. He protected us on our entire journey and among all the nations through which we traveled.—Josh 24:17 (Ex 23:20; Dt 8:2-6)

We are tempted to think that it is not true keeping unless it is in our own way and according to our own ideas. But our Lord himself has taught us that it must be in God's way and not our own, or it would not be true keeping at all.

The devil led him to Jerusalem and had him stand on the highest point of the temple. "If you are the Son of God," he said, "throw

yourself down from here. For it is written:
    " 'He will command his angels concerning you / to guard you
    carefully; / they will lift you up in their hands, / so that you will
    not strike your foot against a stone.' "
Jesus answered, "It says: 'Do not put the Lord your God to the
test.' "—Lk 4:9-12

Only God, who knows the end of things from the beginning, can keep us, and if he shall *seem* to leave us to the will of
our enemies for a time, it is only that he may bring us to a
grander victory in the end.

For we are not to be taken out of the world and its trials, but
are to be kept in the midst of them, and are to be preserved
from the evil that is in them.

> Since you have kept my command to endure patiently, I will also
> keep you from the hour of trial that is going to come upon the
> whole world to test those who live on the earth.
>   —Rv 3:10 (Jn 17:15; Pt 1:5-7)

The divine pathway by which we may enter this heavenly
keep, even while here on earth, is plainly set before us.

> Do not be anxious about anything, but in everything, by prayer
> and petition, with thanksgiving, present your requests to God.
> And the peace of God, which transcends all understanding, will
> guard your hearts and your minds in Christ Jesus.—Phil 4:6-7

We must give up all care of our own, by an utter surrender of
everything to the Divine Caretaker, and by an implicit trust in
him; and then must just simply let him know our wants and our
needs from day to day. And if this is honestly done, and *persisted
in steadfastly,* the result will unfailingly be, that the peace of
God will keep the hearts and minds of all who thus commit
themselves and all they have to his care.

I remember once hearing of a man who thought he could
not live unless he kept himself alive. He was afraid his breath
would stop if he did not keep it going by his own efforts, and
he tried so hard to keep breathing, that he nearly strangled
himself in the struggle. His family in great alarm called in a

physician, who, seeing at once the difficulty, called out to him peremptorily to stop trying to breathe. "I shall die if I do," gasped out the poor man. "Die then," exclaimed the doctor, "but STOP!" The man, overborne by the voice of authority, obeyed, and the moment he stopped trying to breathe, his breath came easily and without effort.

Just so it is with some Christians. They are trying to keep themselves alive, and their life is nearly strangled in the effort. If they would but give up trying to live, and would let Christ keep them alive, they would find themselves living easily and without effort.

THREE

Rest of Soul

Foundation Text. *Come to me, all you who are weary and burdened, and I will give you rest.* —Mt 11:28

There is in every human heart a cry for *rest*. Life at its best in this stage of existence is full of weariness. Both soul and body are "weary and burdened" with their struggles; and humanity makes one long moan for rest.

My heart is in anguish within me; / the terrors of death assail me. / Fear and trembling have beset me; / horror has overwhelmed me. / I said, "Oh, that I had the wings of a dove! / I would fly away and be at rest— / I would flee far away / and stay in the desert; / I would hurry to my place of shelter, / far from the tempest and storm."—Ps 55:4-8

We would gladly "fly away" if we could, but we may not; and therefore the rest our Lord proposes is not a rest *from* the trial and struggle, but a rest *in* it.

Rest in the Lord, and wait patiently for Him; / fret not thyself because of him who prospereth in his way, / because of the man who bringeth wicked devices to pass.—Ps 37:7 (KJV)

It is a rest "in the Lord," not in circumstances, or things, or people, and therefore it takes the "fret" out of life. This divine rest is to the soul what resting in a bed is to the body. We all know the delightful relaxing of every strain that comes to us in bed; the delicious letting go of the whole body in a perfect abandonment of ease and comfort. And just such is the ease of soul that comes from resting "in the Lord."

But this rest implies perfect confidence in him. If one should lie down in a bed that was in any way insecure, and was therefore liable to fall, it would be impossible to let one's self go in an abandonment of rest. We would be compelled to hold on to something else, to keep ourselves safe in such a bed as that. And it must be because Christians do not really believe the Lord alone to be a perfectly secure resting-place, that they seek so eagerly for something else to hold on by; some good feelings, or good works, some church ordinances, or some special and remarkable experiences. What would we think of the folly of a man who should feel afraid his bed could not support him, and should try to hold himself up by ropes attached to the ceiling? And yet this would be nothing compared to the folly of those Christians who say they are resting in Christ, and who yet are holding on to other supports.

> The fruit of righteousness will be peace; / the effect of righteousness will be quietness and confidence forever. / My people will live in peaceful dwelling places, / in undisturbed places of rest.
> —Is 32:17-18

Christ is a resting-place that cannot fail; and to those who have come to him, there ought to be no fear of falling, and no strain to hold one's self safe.

> "My people have been lost sheep; / their shepherds have led them astray / and caused them to roam on the mountains. / They wandered over mountain and hill / and forgot their own resting place."—Jer 50:6

How truly God's people have forgotten their "resting-place." Let the almost universal restlessness of "believers" testify. And the result is as grievous to us now, as it was to Israel of old.

> This is what the Sovereign Lord, the Holy One of Israel, says: / "In repentance and rest in your salvation, / in quietness and trust is your strength, / but you would have none of it. / You said, 'No, we will ride off on swift horses.' / Therefore your pursuers will be swift!—Is 30:15-16 (Is 28:12)

This blessed rest however always awaits God's people, wherever or whoever they may be, and no past unrest can hinder us from entering in.

> There remains, then, a sabbath-rest for the people of God.
> —Heb 4:9 (Jer 30:10)

But this rest can only be entered into by faith. Unbelief effectually, and in the very nature of things, shuts us out.

> And to whom did God swear that they would never enter his rest if not to those who disobeyed? So we see that they were not able to enter, because of their unbelief.
> Therefore, since the promise of entering his rest still stands, let us be careful that none of you be found to have fallen short of it. For we also have had the gospel preached to us, just as they did; but the message they heard was of no value to them, because those who heard did not combine it with faith.—Heb 3:18-19; 4:1-2

Notice the expressions "enter" and "entering." We cannot work for this rest, nor purchase it, nor provide it; we simply "enter into" the rest provided for us by one, who offers himself to us as our resting-place. Just as we rest in a strong and loving earthly friend, who undertakes our case and promises to carry it through, so, only infinitely more, must we rest in the Lord; and it requires faith on our part in both cases alike. If we doubt our friend, we cannot rest, no matter how much we may try; and if we doubt our Lord, we cannot rest either, no matter how much we may try. For rest comes always by trusting, not by trying.

There remains, then, a Sabbath-rest for the people of God; for anyone who enters God's rest also rests from his own work, just as God did from his. Let us, therefore, make every effort to enter that rest, so that no one will fall by following their example of disobedience.—Heb 4:9-11 (Heb 4:3-8)

Making "every effort" to enter into rest is not the effort of work, but the effort of ceasing from our own working. The natural thought of the human heart is, that salvation in everything is to be gained by our own self efforts, and it is indeed an "effort" often to get rid of this.

Refer to the marginal reading on Hebrews 4:9, where rest is rendered "keeping of a Sabbath." This teaches us in type what true soul-rest is.

Thus the heavens and the earth were completed in all their vast array. By the seventh day God had finished the work he had been doing; so on the seventh day he rested from all his work. And God blessed the seventh day and made it holy, because on it he rested from all the work of creating that he had done.—Gn 2:1-3

Then the Lord said to Moses, "Say to the Israelites, 'You must observe my Sabbaths. This will be a sign between me and you for the generations to come, so you may know that I am the Lord, who makes you holy.

" 'Observe the Sabbath, because it is holy to you. Anyone who desecrates it must be put to death; whoever does any work on that day must be cut off from his people. For six days work is to be done, but the seventh day is a Sabbath of rest, holy to the Lord. Whoever does any work on the Sabbath day must be put to death. The Israelites are to observe the Sabbath, celebrating it for the generations to come as a lasting covenant. It will be a sign between me and the Israelites forever, for in six days the Lord made the heavens and the earth, and on the seventh day he abstained from work and rested.' "—Ex 31:12-17

What this outward sabbath was to the children of Israel, the inward keeping of a sabbath is to be to us now. We are to cease from our own works inwardly, as they were to cease outwardly.

Nevertheless, some of the people went out on the seventh day to gather it, but they found none. Then the Lord said to Moses, "How long will you refuse to keep my commands and my instructions? Bear in mind that the sixth day he gives you bread for two days. Everyone is to stay where he is on the seventh day; no one is to go out." So the people rested on the seventh day.
—Ex 16:27-30

The Sabbath was a *gift,* not a *demand.* The Lord had provided the supply for that day, therefore they did not need to seek for any more, but were commanded to rest instead.

While the Israelites were in the desert, a man was found gathering wood on the Sabbath day. Those who found him gathering wood brought him to Moses and Aaron and the whole assembly, and they kept him in custody, because it was not clear what should be done to him. Then the Lord said to Moses, "The man must die. The whole assembly must stone him outside the camp." So the assembly took him outside the camp and stoned him to death, as the Lord commanded Moses.—Nm 15:32-36.

This is a type of the spiritual death which comes upon the soul that breaks God's inward Sabbath of rest, by the spirit of legal dependence upon its own self efforts for salvation.

For anyone who enters God's rest also rests from his own work, just as God did from his.—Heb 4:10

God rested because he had finished his work. We are to rest because the Lord works for us. Everything is provided for us in Christ, and we are to "enter into" the results of his labor, and be at rest.

This is what the Lord says: Be careful not to carry a load on the Sabbath day or bring it through the gates of Jerusalem. Do not bring a load out of your houses or do any work on the Sabbath, but keep the Sabbath day holy, as I commanded your fore-fathers.—Jer 17:21-22

In this inward "keeping of a Sabbath" we are not to bear burdens, because the Lord bears them for us.

> Cast your cares on the Lord / and he will sustain you; / he will never let the righteous fall.—Ps 55:22 (Jer 17:27)

There may arise the natural fear that nothing will be accomplished for the soul that thus keeps a continual inward Sabbath, and bears no burdens. But the answer is full and glorious:

> But if you are careful to obey me, declares the Lord, and bring no load through the gates of this city on the Sabbath, but keep the Sabbath day holy by not doing any work on it, then kings who sit on David's throne will come through the gates of this city with their officials. They and their officials will come riding in chariots and on horses, accompanied by the men of Judah and those living in Jerusalem, and this city will be inhabited forever. People will come from the towns of Judah and the villages around Jerusalem, from the territory of Benjamin and the western foothills, from the hill country and the Negev, bringing burnt offerings and sacrifices, grain offerings, incense and thank offerings to the house of the Lord.—Jer 17:24-26 (Is 58:13-14)

Plentiful blessings, full of richness, come to the soul that thus ceases from its own works, and lets God work for it. When we bear our own burdens and do our own work, deadness and loss are the result; when we rest in the Lord, riches and victory follow.

This is further illustrated in the sabbath of the seventh year which was enjoined upon the Israelites; and the sabbath of the year of jubilee, which occurred every fiftieth year.

> The Lord said to Moses on Mount Sinai, "Speak to the Israelites and say to them: 'When you enter the land I am going to give you, the land itself must observe a sabbath to the Lord. For six years sow your fields, and for six years prune your vineyards and gather their crops. But in the seventh year the land is to have a sabbath of rest, a sabbath to the Lord. Do not sow your fields or

prune your vineyards. Do not reap what grows of itself or harvest the grapes of your untended vines. The land is to have a year of rest.—Lv 25:1-5

" 'Count off seven sabbaths of years—seven times seven years—so that the seven sabbaths of years amount to a period of forty-nine years. . . . Consecrate the fiftieth year and proclaim liberty throughout the land to all its inhabitants. It shall be a jubilee for you; each one of you is to return to his family property and each to his own clan. The fiftieth year shall be a jubilee for you; do not sow and do not reap what grows of itself or harvest the untended vines.—Lv 25:8, 10-11

This typifies the quietude of faith, when the full rest is reached for everything, and when the soul has no need to carry burdens or do work.

You may ask, "What will we eat in the seventh year if we do not plant or harvest our crops?" I will sent you such a blessing in the sixth year that the land will yield enough for three years. While you plant during the eighth year, you will eat from the old crop and will continue to eat from it until the harvest of the ninth year comes in."—Lv 25:20-22

Notice the question of unbelief in verse 20, "What will we eat?" and the answer in verse 22, "You will eat from the old crop." This is a type of the store that is laid up for us in Christ, who is made for us "wisdom and righteousness and sanctification and redemption." Whatever the land yields during the sabbath year will be food for you." (Lv 25:6)

In divine things our "keeping of sabbaths" brings to us our richest blessings. Our very rest is "food" for us, and for all who belong to us. Moreover our resting is a "feast" to the Lord.

"Speak to the Israelites and say to them: 'These are my appointed feasts, the appointed feasts of the Lord, which you are to proclaim as sacred assemblies.

" 'There are six days when you may work, but the seventh day is a Sabbath of rest, a day of sacred assembly. You are not to do any work; wherever you live, it is a Sabbath to the Lord.' "—Lv 23:2-3

On the days of the Lord's feasts, no work was to be done. Notice the expression so frequently used in this twenty-third chapter of Leviticus, "You are not to do any work" (see verses 7, 8, 21, 25, 35, 36). There are many Christians who try to keep the feasts of the Lord by doing "work"; work which is done from duty only, and not from love; work which is a "great cross" and a "heavy burden," and which would not be done at all, if the soul could hope to get to heaven by any other pathway.

> I will destroy from among his people anyone who does any work on that day. You shall do no work at all. This is to be a lasting ordinance for the generations to come, wherever you live. It is a sabbath of rest for you.—Lv 23:30-32

We cannot feast while those we love are toiling; and neither can our God.

> David said to Solomon: "My son, I had it in my heart to build a house for the Name of the Lord my God. But this word of the Lord came to me: 'You have shed much blood and have fought many wars. You are not to build a house for my Name, because you have shed much blood on the earth in my sight. But you will have a son who will be a man of peace and rest, and I will give him rest from all his enemies on every side. His name will be Solomon, and I will grant Israel peace and quiet during his reign. He is the one who will build a house for my Name. He will be my son, and I will be his father. And I will establish the throne of his kingdom over Israel forever.'"—1 Chr 22:8-10

The Lord cannot make his abode in the midst of conflict and unrest; and we cannot know his abiding presence in the inward temple of our hearts, while our experience is only one of conflict. An interior rest must be realized before this inward divine union can be known (see 1 Chr 22:17-19; Dt 12:9-11).
The Lord rests when we rest.

> For the Lord has chosen Zion, / he has desired it for his dwelling: / "This is my resting place for ever and ever; / here I will sit enthroned, for I have desired it."—Ps 132:13-14 (2 Chr 6:41)

A mother cannot rest while her little ones are toiling or bearing burdens. She must see them all at rest before she herself can be comfortable. And just so it is with our God.

There are two conditions to soul-rest expressed in the two following verses:

> "Take my yoke upon you and learn from me, for I am gentle and humble in heart, and you will find rest for your souls."—Mt 11:29
>
> Now we who have believed enter that rest.—Heb 4:3a

Surrender, faith, and obedience are necessary at every step of the divine progress, and nowhere more necessary than here. Without them rest is simply impossible, in the very nature of things. The little child rests in its mother, only when it yields unquestioning submission to her control, and trusts implicitly in her love. The ox that yields to the yoke without chafing, rests under it; while the young bullock, "unaccustomed to the yoke," finds it a galling burden. Truly many Christians have less sense than the dumb animals; for the animals, when they find the yoke inevitable, yield to it and it becomes easy, while we are tempted to chafe and worry under it as long as life lasts.

Learn to "take" the yoke upon you. Do not wait for it to be forced on you; but bow your neck to it willingly, and "take" it. Say *"Yes, Lord"* to each expression of his will in all the circumstances of your lives. Say it with full consent to everything; to the loss of your money, or the loss of your health, or to the malice of enemies or the cruelty of friends. Take each yoke as it comes, and in the taking you will find rest.

Notice the expressions in Matthew 11:28-29, "I will *give* you rest," and "you will *find* rest." This rest cannot be earned, nor bought, nor attained. It is simply *given* by God, and *found* by us. And all who thus come to Christ in the way of surrender and trust, "find" it without any effort. They "enter into rest." For in his presence there is never any unrest.

> The Lord replied, "My Presence will go with you, and I will give you rest."—Ex 33:14

The mere presence of the mother is perfect rest to the infant, no matter what tumult or danger may surround it. And, if we only knew him, God's presence would be perfect rest to us.

When He giveth quietness, who then can make trouble?
—Jb 34:29 (KJV)

Among the peaks of the Sierra Nevada mountains, not far from the busy whirl of San Francisco, the great metropolis of the Pacific coast, lies Lake Tahoe. It is twenty-three miles long, ten miles wide, and so deep that the line at 1,900 feet does not touch bottom; and it lies 5,000 thousand feet above the neighbouring ocean. Storms come and go in lower waters, but this lake the while is so still and its water so clear that the eye can penetrate, it is said, a hundred feet into its depths. A bell can be heard for ten or twenty miles. Around its mild verdant sides are the mountains, ever crowned with snow. The sky above is as calm as the motionless water. Nature loses scarcely anything of its clear outline as it is reflected there. Here the soul may learn something of what *rest* is, as day after day one opens one's heart to let the sweet influences of nature's sabbath enter and reign. And this is but a faint type of what we may find in Christ.

In the pressure of the greatest responsibilities, in the worry of the smallest cares, in the perplexity of life's moments of crisis, we may have the Lake Tahoe rest in the fastnesses of God's will. Learn to live in this rest; and in the calm of spirit which it will give, your soul will reflect as in a mirror the "beauty of the Lord," and the tumult of men's lives will be calmed in your presence as your tumults have been calmed in the presence of God.

The fruit of righteousness will be peace; / the effect of righteousness will be quietness and confidence forever. / My people will live in peaceful dwelling places, / in secure homes, / in undisturbed places of rest.—Is 32:17-18

FOUR

Surrendering to the Will of God

Foundation Text— *Therefore, I urge you, brothers, in view of God's mercy, to offer your bodies as living sacrifices, holy and pleasing to God—which is your spiritual worship. Do not conform any longer to the pattern of this world, but be transformed by the renewing of your mind. Then you will be able to test and approve what God's will is—his good, pleasing and perfect will.* —Rom 12:1-2

However widely Christians may differ on other subjects, however divergent may be their "views" of truth or of doctrine, there is one point upon which every thoughtful soul will agree; and that is, the fact that we all, without reference to our "views" or "doctrines," are called to an entire surrender of ourselves to the will of God. We are made for union with him, and the only pathway to this must of course be a perfect harmony between our will and his. For "how *can* two walk together except they be agreed?"

Therefore God's commands to us to be holy, are all based upon the fact that he to whom we belong is holy.

> But just as he who called you is holy, so be holy in all you do; for it is written: "Be holy, because I am holy."
> —1 Pt 1:15-16 (Lv 11:44-45)

In order to be one with him, which is our final destiny, we must be like him in character; and since he is holy, we cannot be "partakers of his nature," without ourselves being holy also.

> The Lord said to Moses, "Speak to the entire assembly of Israel and say to them: 'Be holy because I, the Lord your God am holy.'"—Lv 19:1-2

> "'Consecrate yourselves and be holy, because I am the Lord your God. Keep my decrees and follow them. I am the Lord, who makes you holy.'"—Lv 20:7-8

It is because we *are* the Lord's, and not in order that we may become his, that we are called to be holy. "I am the Lord your God," is always the ground of the appeal. Not, "I will be your God, if you will be holy," but "Be holy because I *am* the Lord your God."

Notice the "therefores" in this connection.

> You were bought at a price. Therefore honor God with your body.—1 Cor 6:20 (2 Cor 7:1)

It is because we *have been* bought with a price, and not in order to induce our Lord to buy us, that we are urged to holiness.

> How great is the love the Father has lavished on us, that we should be called children of God! And that is what we are! The reason the world does not know us is that it did not know him. Dear friends, now we are children of God, and what we will be has not yet been made known. But we know that when he appears, we shall be like him, for we shall see him as he is. Everyone who has this hope in him purifies himself, just as he is pure.—1 Jn 3:1-3

Having such a hope as this of being one day like him, we are incited now to purify ourselves even as he is pure.

The preliminary step to consecration, therefore, must be to settle once for all the question of whether we belong to the Lord or not, and whether the promises of the gospel are really ours. And then, when this is settled, let us "therefore" present ourselves in glad and loving surrender to the divine Master who laid down his life to make us his own.

The children of Israel were not called upon to consecrate themselves until after they were saved from Egypt. The law could not be given while they were in bondage to Pharaoh. Therefore in their history, which is a wonderful type of our spiritual life, they came to consecration only after many other steps had been taken.

We can trace these steps in the four books of Exodus, Leviticus, Numbers, and Deuteronomy.

In Exodus they came out of Egypt—answering to our deliverance from the bondage of sin.

In Leviticus they received the commands of God as to how they should order their worship and their lives in the land of promise into which God was leading them.

In Numbers they failed through unbelief to enter into the promised land, and in consequence wandered in the wilderness forty years—answering to the common Christian experience of failure and wandering.

In Deuteronomy they came a second time to the borders of the land and were called to an entire consecration before they could enter in. The commands of God were rehearsed by Moses, and they were asked if they would keep and do them; and this is therefore the book of consecration.

> Hear now, O Israel, the decrees and laws I am about to teach you. Follow them so that you may live and may go in and take possession of the land that the Lord, the God of your fathers, is giving you. Do not add to what I command you and do not subtract from it, but keep the commands of the Lord your God that I give you.—Dt 4:1-2

> And now, O Israel, what does the Lord your God ask of you but to fear the Lord your God, to walk in all his ways, to love him, to serve the Lord your God with all your heart and with all your soul, and to observe the Lord's commands and decrees that I am giving you today for your own good?—Dt 10:12-13 (Dt 6:1-3)

Consecration means just what the book of Deuteronomy teaches, that we should surrender ourselves to the Lord, to hear, and keep, and do his will. It means the choosing of his will before everything else. It means saying yes to him throughout the whole range of our being. It means the leaving of one's whole self in his hands, to be dealt with as he shall please. It means the surrender of all liberty of choice, except the liberty to choose his will and his way.

> Anyone who loves his father or mother more than me is not worthy of me; anyone who loves his son or daughter more than me is not worthy of me; and anyone who does not take his cross and follow me is not worthy of me. Whoever finds his life will lose it, and whoever loses his life for my sake will find it. —Mt 10:37-39

> Then Jesus said to his disciples, "If anyone would come after me, he must deny himself and take up his cross and follow me. For whoever wants to save his life will lose it, but whoever loses his life for me will find it. What good will it be for a man if he gains the whole world, yet forfeits his soul? Or what can a man give in exchange for his soul?"—Mt 16:24-26 (Lk 14:26-33)

In these passages our Lord himself tells us what consecration means. And in another passage he shows us that it must not be a pretense, a consecration of words only, nor even a consecration of religious service only; but that it must be a reality, in the daily *doing* of the will of God.

> Not everyone who says to me, "Lord, Lord," will enter the kingdom of heaven, but only he who does the will of my Father who is in heaven. Many will say to me on that day, "Lord, Lord, did we not prophesy in your name, and in your name drive out demons and perform many miracles?" Then I will tell them plainly, "I never knew you. Away from me, you evildoers!"
> —Mt 7:21-23

God's purpose in our redemption was our entire consecration. Christians too often look upon consecration as something extra added on to salvation, not necessarily an essential part; and therefore think it is optional with them to enter into it or not, as they may please. Whereas the Bible declares that salvation is nothing, if it does not ultimately lead to holiness; for salvation in God's thought *is* holiness.

> "She will give birth to a son, and you are to give him the name Jesus, because he will save his people from their sins."—Mt 1:21

> For the grace of God that brings salvation has appeared to all men. It teaches us to say "No" to ungodliness and worldly passions, and to live self-controlled, upright and godly lives in this present age, while we wait for the blessed hope—the glorious appearing of our great god and Savior, Jesus Christ, who gave himself for us to redeem us from all wickedness and to purify for himself a people that are his very own, eager to do what is good.
> —Ti 2:11-14 (Lk 1:68-75; Acts 3:26)

It is very striking to notice that of the many announcements made concerning the work Christ came to accomplish, nearly every one declares it to be the deliverance from *sin,* rather than the escape of *punishment.* It is a salvation to *holiness,* rather than a salvation to *heaven.* Of course punishment is escaped, and heaven is gained, in the nature of things, when we are saved from sin; since the greater always involves the less. But the vital thing in the redemption of Christ is evidently to redeem "from all wickedness," and "purify for himself a people that are his very own, eager to do what is good."

> The Lord said, "I have indeed seen the misery of my people in Egypt. I have heard them crying out because of their slave drivers, and I am concerned about their suffering. So I have come down to rescue them from the hand of the Egyptians and to bring them up out of that land into a good and spacious land, a land flowing with milk and honey."—Ex 3:7-8

The thought of God in the deliverance of Israel was not that they should wander in the wilderness, but that they should be brought into the promised land; which land typifies the life of full consecration.

Entire consecration therefore is binding upon every Christian, and sooner or later each one must come to know it.

> Make every effort to live in peace with all men and to be holy; without holiness no one will see the Lord.—Heb 12:14

Our Lord teaches us this in the contrast he draws between the house built on the rock, and the one built on the sand.

> Therefore everyone who hears these words of mine and puts them into practice is like a wise man who built his house on the rock. The rain came down, the streams rose, and the winds blew and beat against that house; yet it did not fall, because it had its foundation on the rock. But everyone who hears these words of mine and does not put them into practice is like a foolish man who built his house on sand. The rain came down, the streams rose, and the winds blew and beat against that house, and it fell with a great crash.—Mt 7:24-27

"Building on the rock" here evidently means the hearing and doing the will of God; while "building on the sand" was the hearing but doing it not. The contrast was between consecration and no consecration. There is therefore no alternative. If we would have our house to stand, we *must* be consecrated, for without consecration it will fall, and great will be the fall of it.

In the 28th chapter of Deuteronomy we have a striking confirmation of this, in the contrast drawn between those who "obey the Lord and carefully follow all his commands," and those who will "not obey the Lord."

> If you fully obey the Lord your God and carefully follow all his commands I give you today, the Lord your God will set you high above all the nations on earth. All these blessings will come upon you and accompany you if you obey the Lord your God.
> You will be blessed in the city and blessed in the country.
> The fruit of your womb will be blessed, and the crops of your land and the young of your livestock—the calves of your herds and the lambs of your flocks.

Your basket and your kneading trough will be blessed.
You will be blessed when you come in and blessed when you go out—Dt 28:1-6

However, if you do not obey the Lord your God and do not carefully follow all his commands and decrees I am giving you today, all these curses will come upon you and overtake you:

You will be cursed in the city and cursed in the country. / Your basket and your kneading trough will be cursed. / The fruit of your womb will be cursed, and the crops of your land, and the calves of your herds and the lambs of your flocks. / You will be cursed when you come in and cursed when you go out.
—Dt 28:15-19

It is deeply interesting to read the whole chapter through with this contrast in mind. We should make a spiritual application of the blessings and curses spoken of. Our enemies are spiritual enemies; our possessions are spiritual riches; our sight or our blindness are the sight or blindness of the soul; our diseases are the diseases of sin; our hunger and nakedness are spiritual; and our bondage is the bondage of the spirit. As a matter of fact every Christian can testify to the truth of one or the other of these descriptions. Those who know what it is to be consecrated, know also that the promised blessings have been theirs; and on the other hand those who have not consecrated themselves, know only too well how much of the consequent loss and failure have come into their spiritual lives.

Consecration brings the soul into relations of infinite blessedness to the Lord.

"Whoever has my commands and obeys them, he is the one who loves me. He who loves me will be loved by my Father, and I too will love him and show myself to him."
Then Judas (not Judas Iscariot) said, "But, Lord, why do you intend to show yourself to us and not to the world?"
Jesus replied, "If anyone loves me, he will obey my teaching. My Father will love him, and we will come to him and make our home with him. He who does not love me will not obey my teaching.

These words you hear are not my own; they belong to the Father who sent me."—Jn 14:21-24

You are my friends if you do what I command.—Jn 15:14

Whoever does God's will is my brother and sister and mother.
—Mk 3:35

To be his "friends," to know his conscious indwelling presence, to be as it were his "brother and sister and mother," all these things are surely full of unspeakable worth to our souls.

As Jesus was saying these things, a woman in the crowd called out, "Blessed is the mother who gave you birth and nursed you."
He replied, "Blessed rather are those who hear the word of God and obey it."—Lk 11:27-28

We may have wished often, in our love for our divine Master, that we could have held him in our arms and pressed him to our bosoms, but here we see that a present life of consecration is more to be desired than even this.

Now if you obey me fully and keep my covenant, then out of all nations you will be my treasured possession. Although the whole earth is mine, you will be for me a kingdom of priests and a holy nation.—Ex 19:5-6

Only a consecrated soul can know the joy of being God's "treasured possession." And only a consecrated soul can know clearly the will of God, for obedience is the universal key to knowledge.

If any one chooses to do God's will, he will find out whether my teaching comes from God or whether I speak on my own.
—Jn 7:17

The Lord confides in those who fear him; / he makes his covenant known to them.—Ps 25:14

Consecration brings rejoicing. At the first sight of it, the soul shrinks and is afraid; but when it has looked more deeply into the beauty and blessedness of the will of God, it learns to rejoice. This was the case of the Israelites in Nehemiah's time (Neh 8:8-10, 12).

After a time of long backsliding on the part of the children of Israel, during which the book of God's law had been lost sight of, it was found again, and the people had all been assembled in the public square of the city to hear it read. At first they wept, but as they understood it better, they saw it was a cause of rejoicing and not of sorrow, and they celebrated "with great joy because they now understood the words that had been made known to them."

God's will is always our highest joy. He would have us always to "be joyful at our feasts."

> Remember that you were slaves in Egypt, and follow carefully these decrees.
> Celebrate the Feast of Tabernacles for seven days after you have gathered the produce of your threshing floor and your winepress. Be joyful at your Feast—you, your sons and daughters, your menservants and maidservants, and the Levites, the aliens, the fatherless and the widows who live in your towns. For seven days celebrate the Feast to the Lord your God at the place the Lord will choose. For the Lord your God will bless you in all your harvest and in all the work of your hands, and your joy will be complete.
> —Dt 16:12-15

In fact, how can we do other than love the will of our God when we become acquainted with him, and learn to know that his will is the will of infinite love and must be therefore infinitely lovely. No most loving mother's will for her child was ever half so lovely as this sweet beloved will of our God for us. It is something to delight in, instead of to fear; and the words "Thy will be done," when once we understand them, become the dearest words our lips can utter.

> Then I said, "Lo, I come; / in the roll of the book it is written of me; / I delight to do thy will, O my God; / thy law is within my heart."—Ps 40:7-8 (RSV)

"My food," said Jesus, "is to do the will of him who sent me and to finish his work."—Jn 4:34

Do we "delight" to do God's will? Is it our "food" to do it? We need to watch against a grudging service. The enemy is always trying to get in the word duty instead of the word delight; he says a stern "you must" instead of the loving "you cmay." When a mother cares for her child from duty only, the tender sweetness of the mother love has gone. When the husband or wife begin to say "I ought" instead of "I delight to" in their relationship with the other, the home becomes a prison. There is no slavery like the slavery of love, but its chains are sweet. It knows nothing of "sacrifice," no matter what may be given up. It "delights to do the will" of the beloved one.

Our Lord can never be satisfied until this is the attitude of our souls towards him. His purposes of grace for us are that there should be harmony between our wills and his: not two wills crossing one another, but two wills made one.

Has it become so with us as yet; can we say that it is our "food" to do his will?

If not, the choice is before us now, and we must decide it.

See, I am setting before you today a blessing and a curse—the blessing if you obey the commands of the Lord your God that I am giving you today; the curse if you disobey the commands of the Lord your God and turn from the way that I command you today by following other gods, which you have not known.
—Dt 11:26-28

May the Lord enable us to settle the question at once and forever on the side of his will and not our own!

The process of consecration is shown us in Deuteronomy.

The Lord your God commands you this day to follow these decrees and laws; carefully observe them with all your heart and with all your soul. You have declared this day that the Lord is your God and that you will walk in his ways, that you will keep his decrees, commands and laws, and that you will obey him. And the Lord has declared this day that you are his people, his treasured possession as he promised, and that you are to keep all his commands. He has declared that he will set you in praise, fame and honor high above all the nations he has made and that you will be a people holy to the Lord your God, as he promised. —Dt 26:16-19

First, God's command in verse sixteen.
Second, our surrender in verse seventeen.
Third, God's response in verses eighteen and nineteen.

When we have heard the call to surrender, and have declared the Lord to be our God, and that we *will* walk in his ways and keep his commandments, He always declared us to be his people, and declares that he will make us holy. And from that moment, he takes full possession of us. What *can* he do but take possession of the soul, that surrenders itself to him? And of course he sanctifies that which is thus his own. The law of offerings to the Lord settles this as a primary fact, that everything which is given to him, becomes by that very act something holy, set apart from all other things for his use alone.

> But nothing that a man owns and devotes to the Lord— whether man or animal or family land—may be sold or redeemed; everything so devoted is most holy to the Lord. —Lv 27:28

Having once given it to the Lord, the devoted thing thenceforth was reckoned by all Israel as being his, and no one dared stretch forth a hand to retake it.

> He must not pick out the good from the bad or make any substitution. If he does make a substitution, both the animal and its substitute become holy and cannot be redeemed. —Lv 27:33

The giver might have felt his offering to be a very poor one, or to have been very poorly made; but having made it, the matter was taken out of his hands altogether, and the devoted thing, by God's own law, became "most holy to the Lord." It was not the intention of the giver nor the quality of the gift that made it holy, but the holiness of the receiver. God's possession of anything sanctifies it. "The altar sanctifies the gift."

Having consecrated ourselves therefore to the Lord, we must from that moment reckon always that we *are* the Lord's, no matter what the "seemings" may be. We must refuse to admit a question or a doubt, but must choose always with an unfaltering purpose of heart to have no will but the will of God. We may not always *feel* as if we were consecrated, but we may always *choose* to be, and it is the attitude of our will, and not the state of our emotions, that is the vital thing in our soul life. If in my will I choose to be all the Lord's, then it is a fact that I *am* all his, no matter how I may feel about it. We need therefore to attend only to the state of the will in this matter of consecration.

Let us make then a hearty renunciation of our wills to God, and let us from this time onward accept his will as our only portion.

I believe it is safest to come to a definite point in this matter, and to make a definite transaction of it.

A great many Christians acknowledge that they ought to do it, and are always meaning to do it; but because they do not come to the definite point of doing it, it is never really done. I may want and intend to give a gift to a friend with all the earnestness possible, but until I come to the point of actually giving it, it will still remain in my own possession.

If we mean to obey the command with which our lesson opens, when could we find a better time than now? Every hour that we delay we are holding ourselves back from blessing, and are grieving the heart of our Lord.

Now, who is willing to consecrate himself today to the Lord?
—1 Chr 29:5

Laid on thine altar, Oh my Lord divine,
Accept my gift this day, for Jesus' sake;—
I have no jewels to adorn thy shrine,
Nor any world-famed sacrifice to make,—
But here I bring within my trembling hand

This will of mine,—a thing that seemeth small,
And only thou, sweet Lord, canst understand
How, when I yield thee this, I yield *mine all*!
Hidden therein, thy searching eye can see
Struggles of passion, visions of delight,
All that I love, or am, or fain would be,—
Deep loves, fond hopes, and longings infinite.
It hath been wet with tears and dimmed with sighs,
Clenched in my grasp, till beauty it hath none.
Now from thy footstool, where it vanquished lies,
The prayer ascendeth, May thy will be done.
Take it, oh Father, ere my courage fail;
And merge it so in thine own will, that e'en
If in some desperate hour my cries prevail,
And thou give back my gift, it may have been
So changed, so purified, so fair have grown,
So one with thee, so filled with peace divine,
I may not know or feel it as mine *own*,
But, gaining back my will, may find it *thine*.

FIVE

Have No Anxiety

Foundation Text— *Have no anxiety about anything, but in everything by prayer and supplication with thanksgiving let your requests be made known to God. And the peace of God, which passes all understanding, will keep your hearts and your minds in Christ Jesus.* —Phil 4:6-7 (RSV)

Notice the phrase "have no anxiety" as covering all possible grounds for anxiety, both inward and outward. We are continually tempted to think it is our duty to be anxious about some things. Perhaps our thought will be, "Oh yes, it is quite right to give up all anxiety in a general way; and in spiritual matters of course anxiety is wrong; but there *are* things about which it would be a sin not to be anxious—about our children, for instance, or those we love, or about our church affairs and the cause of truth, or about our business matters. It would show a great lack of concern not to be anxious about such things as these." Or else our thoughts take the other tack, and we say to ourselves, "Yes, it is quite right to commit our loved ones and all our outward affairs to the Lord, but when it comes to our inward lives, our religious experiences, our temptations, our besetting sins, our growth in grace, and all such things, these we *ought* to be anxious about, for if we are not, they will be sure to be neglected."

49

To such suggestions and to all similar ones, the answer is found in our text—"Have no anxiety."

There is no getting away from this upon any subterfuge whatever. All the circumstances may call for an apparently rightful anxiety, but God knows, and he says "have no anxiety," and that settles it forever.

Our Lord develops this, and shows us the reason why we are not to be anxious, in his sermon on the mount.

> Therefore I tell you, do not worry about your life, what you will eat or drink; or about your body, what you will wear. Is not life more important than clothes? Look at the birds of the air; they do not sow or reap or store away in barns, and yet your heavenly Father feeds them. Are you not much more valuable than they? Who of you by worrying can add a single hour to his life?
>
> And why do you worry about clothes? See how the lilies of the field grow. They do not labor or spin. Yet I tell you that not even Solomon in all his splendor was dressed like one of these. If that is how God clothes the grass of the field, which is here today and tomorrow is thrown into the fire, will he not much more clothe you, O you of little faith? So do not worry, saying "What shall we drink?" or "What shall we wear?" For the pagans run after all these things, and your heavenly Father knows that you need them. But seek first his kingdom and his righteousness, and all these things will be given to you as well. Therefore do not worry about tomorrow, for tomorrow will worry about itself. Each day has enough trouble of its own.—Mt 6:25-34

The illustrations here cannot be misunderstood. The birds and the flowers are before us continually, as living examples of what real trust is. With them of course it is unconscious trust, but with us it must be an intelligent and conscious act. One who had learned this lesson, thus writes concerning it.

"Long years ago I was in the act of kneeling down before the Lord my God, when a little bird in the lightest, freest humor, came and perched near my window, and thus preached to me, all the while hopping from spray to spray, 'Oh thou grave man, look on me and learn something. Thy God made me, and if thou canst conceive it, he loves me, and cares for me. Thou studiest him in great problems which oppress and confound thee, and thou losest sight of one-half of his ways. Learn to see thy God, not in great mysteries only, but in me also. His burden on me is light, his yoke on me is easy, for I have only to submit to him and trust. But thou makest yokes and burdens for thyself, which are grievous to be borne, because thou wilt neither submit nor trust. I advise thee to follow my example, as thy Master commanded thee to do. Consider that the bird and the flower are as really from God as thou art; and that their lives are figures of something which he wants to see in thee also. Behold the fowls of the air, for they sow not, neither do they reap, nor gather into barns; yet your Heavenly Father feedeth them?"

> Humble yourselves, therefore, under God's mighty hand, that he may lift you up in due time. Cast all your anxiety on him because he cares for you.—1 Pt 5:6-7 (Ps 55:22)

We all know the relief it is to give over a care or a burden to a friend whom we trust. And just like this, only infinitely greater, is the relief that comes to the soul that has "cast all its anxiety upon the Lord."

Most Christians act like the man in the story who was walking along a road bowed down under a heavy burden, and was invited to ride by kind friends, passing in a wagon. He accepted the invitation, but still kept the load on his shoulders, and when asked by his friend why he did not lay it on the floor of the wagon, replied: "Oh, it is a great deal to ask of you to carry me; I could not think of asking you to carry my burden too!"

"I have bestowed strength on a warrior."—Ps 89:19

That is, he, upon whom our cares are to be cast, is able to bear them, no matter how great they may be. And yet we, who trust our choicest things often to our fellow-men and feel no fear, are afraid to trust our Lord (Is 12-14; 41:10-11).

Strengthen the feeble hands, / steady the knees that give way; / say to those with fearful hearts, / "Be strong, do not fear; / your God will come, / he will come with vengeance; / with divine retribution / he will come to save you.—Is 35:3-4

So do not fear, for I am with you; / do not be dismayed, for I am your God. / All who rage against you / will surely be ashamed and disgraced; / those who oppose you / will be as nothing and perish.—Is 41:10-11 (Is 12-14)

Think of the blessed confidence with which children cast their cares off upon their parents, without a fear, and recall how the parents love to have it so. How often a mother, when her child is tempted to be anxious or worried over something will say, "There, darling, do not worry; leave it all to me, and I will attend to it. Only trust me, and do as I say, and all will come right."

The only thing that a mother asks of her child is that it will yield to her care and obey her voice, and then she will take charge of all the rest. And just so it is with us and our God.

If you are willing and obedient, you will eat the best from the land.—Is 1:19 (Jer 42:5-6; Dt 5:27-29)

No mother *can* make all things go right for a disobedient child, and neither can God, in the very nature of things.

"But my people would not listen to me; / Israel would not submit to me. / So I gave them over to their stubborn hearts / to follow their own devices.—Ps 81:11-12

If we *will* carry our own cards, and manage things in our own way, and follow "our own devices," sorrow and suffering cannot fail to be the result.

Trust in the Lord with all your heart / and lean not on your own understanding; / in all your ways acknowledge him, / and he will make your paths straight.—Prv 3:5-6

A little girl I knew, once brought a bag without a string to her mother to have one supplied. The mother agreed to do it and began to push the thread through the hem. The child had expected her mother to sew the string on at each side of the bag like a handle, and when she saw the string disappearing inside the hem, she was puzzled and distressed. She watched it a moment, and then said plaintively, "I think my mamma *should* put a string in my bag when she said she would." The mother looked up from her work reassuringly and said, "Do not be troubled, darling, I am putting the string in all right." The child watched silently for a few more moments, and still no sign of the string appearing, as it was a little difficult to push through the narrow hem, the tears began to gather, and again the plaintive voice whispered, "I *thought* my mamma was a good mamma, who knew how to put on strings!" This time the mother saw there was a real need of comfort, and she explained more fully. "See, darling," she said, "I do know how, and this is the best way. Just trust me and wait, and it will all come out right."

The child waited, and in a few moments the string was pushed through, a knot was tied, and the bag hung triumphantly on the little arm. The child looked thoughtfully at it, and then said, "Oh I see. It is just like Jesus. We give him something to do, and he don't seem to be doing it right, and we are just going to worry; and then we think, 'Oh' Jesus knows how'; and we just trust him and wait, and it comes out all right at last."

> Unless the Lord builds the house, / its builders labor in vain. / Unless the Lord watches over the city, / the watchmen stand guard in vain. / In vain you rise early / and stay up late, / toiling for food to eat— / for he grants sleep to those he loves.
> —Ps 127:1-2

All our care is vain unless the Lord shall take the care also. And our worry is all a waste if he does take it. If a mother sits up late and rises early in order to bear her child's burdens, it is so that the child may rest; and it would grieve her sorely to have the child also try to carry the burdens.

> Do not let your hearts be troubled. Trust in God; trust also in me.... Peace I leave with you; my peace I give you. I do not give to you as the world gives. Do not let your hearts be troubled and do not be afraid.—Jn 14:1, 27

Here the Master *commands* us not to be troubled or afraid. So that every time we yield to anxiety or fear we are disobeying him.

There are three instances recorded where our Lord rebuked the little faith of his disciples; and yet in each case the circumstances were such that anxiety seemed the natural and proper thing. Similar circumstances would cause great anxiety in many Christian hearts today.

First it was in a storm at sea.

> Without warning, a furious storm came up on the lake, so that the waves swept over the boat. But Jesus was sleeping. The disciples went and woke him, saying, "Lord, save us! We're going to drown!"
>
> He replied, "You of little faith, why are you so afraid?" Then he got up and rebuked the winds and the waves, and it was completely calm.—Mt 8:24-26

Their fear led them to cry to him, but they ought to have known that, with him aboard, they could not be other than safe, and they ought to have rested in quiet confidence through the storm.

The second instance was when Peter found himself sinking in the waters.

> Then Peter got down out of the boat and walked on the water to Jesus. But when he saw the wind, he was afraid and, beginning to sink, cried out, "Lord, save me!"
>
> Immediately Jesus reached out his hand and caught him. "You of little faith," he said, "why did you doubt?"—Mt 14:29-31

The third was when the disciples were troubled because they had no bread.

Aware of their discussion, Jesus asked, "You of little faith, why are you talking among yourselves about having no bread? Do you still not understand? Don't you remember the five loaves for the five thousand, and how many basketfuls you gathered? Or the seven loaves for the four thousand, and how many basketfuls you gathered?—Mt 16:8-10

Here Jesus refers them to past experiences, when he had supplied all their needs, as a reason why they should trust him now. And I am sure he was grieved at the doubts of his disciples, just as we are grieved when those whom we love and whom we are trying to serve, are anxious and fearful about the things we have undertaken to do for them.

Three instances from the Old Testament will illustrate our lesson. The first is the story of Hagar when she was sent out from her home into the wilderness, apparently to die.

Early the next morning Abraham took some food and a skin of water and gave them to Hagar. He set them on her shoulders and then sent her off with the boy. She went on her way and wandered in the desert of Beersheba.

When the water in the skin was gone, she put the boy under one of the bushes. Then she went off and sat down nearby, about a bowshot away, for she thought, "I cannot watch the boy die." And as she sat there nearby, she began to sob.

God heard the boy crying, and the angel of God called to Hagar from heaven and said to her, "What is the matter, Hagar? Do not be afraid; God has heard the boy crying as he lies there. Lift the boy up and take him by the hand, for I will make him into a great nation."

Then God opened her eyes and she saw a well of water. So she went and filled the skin with water and gave the boy a drink.
—Gn 21:14-19

The second was when Elijah went, during the time of famine, to the house of the widow.

So he went to Zarephath. When he came to the town gate, a widow was there gathering sticks. He called to her and asked,

"Would you bring me a little water in a jar so I may have a drink?" As she was going to get it, he called, "And bring me, please, a piece of bread."

As surely as the Lord your God lives," she replied, "I don't have any bread—only a handful of flour in a jar and a little oil in a jug. I am gathering a few sticks to take home and make a meal for myself and my son, that we may eat it—and die."

Elijah said to her, "Don't be afraid. Go home and do as you have said. But first make a small cake of bread for me from what you have and bring it to me, and then make something for yourself and your son. For this is what the Lord, the God of Israel, says: 'The jar of flour will not be used up and the jug of oil will not run dry until the day the Lord gives rain on the land.' "

She went away and did as Elijah had told her. So there was food every day for Elijah and for the woman and her family. For the jar of flour was not used up and the jug of oil did not run dry, in keeping with the word of the Lord spoken by Elijah.

—1 Kgs 17:10-16

The third was when the army of Syria encompassed the city where dwelt the man of God.

When the servant of the man of God got up and went out early the next morning, an army with horses and chariots had surrounded the city. "Oh, my lord, what shall we do?" the servant asked.

"Don't be afraid," the prophet answered. "Those who are with us are more than those who are with them."

And Elisha prayed, "O Lord, open his eyes so he may see." Then the Lord opened the servant's eyes, and he looked and saw the hills full of horses and chariots of fire all around Elisha.

—2 Kgs 6:15-17

The *causes* for anxiety in each of these cases were very great, but God was in each instance behind the scene with his perfect supply, and those who were afraid only needed to have their eyes opened to see it, and be delivered from all their fears.

What then is our part in this matter?

Trust in the Lord and do good; / dwell in the land and enjoy safe pasture. / Delight yourself in the Lord / and he will give you the desires of your heart. / Commit your way to the Lord; / trust in him and he will do this: / He will make your righteousness shine like the dawn, / the justice of your cause like the noonday sun. / Be still before the Lord and wait patiently for him; / do not fret when men succeed in their ways, / when they carry out their wicked schemes.—Ps 37:3-7

Seven things are mentioned here. Trust in the Lord; do good; delight yourself in him; commit your way to him; be still before him; wait patiently for him; and finally, do not fret yourself.

So do not worry, saying, "What shall we eat?" or "What shall we drink?" or "What shall we wear?" For the pagans run after all these things, and your heavenly Father knows that you need them. But seek first his kingdom and his righteousness, and all these things will be given to you as well.—Mt 6:31-33

Our part then is to seek first the kingdom of God and his righteousness. That is, we must make it the first object of our lives to accept his will and to do it under all circumstances, and then simply trust him for all the rest. No one can in the very nature of things, be free of anxiety, who is not fully surrendered to the Lord; for unless we are satisfied with his will, we cannot trust him to manage for us.

If my people would but listen to me, / if Israel would follow my ways, / how quickly would I subdue their enemies / and turn my hand against their foes! / Those who hate the Lord would cringe before him, / and their punishment would last forever. / But you would be fed with the finest of wheat; / with honey from the rock I would satisfy you.—Ps 81:13-16

There is no way but the way of full surrender and simple childlike obedience. The Lord knows what is best, we do not; therefore we must leave the arrangements all to him, and must say, "Thy will be done," about everything.

Remember, that all questioning is of the nature of doubt. It is called in the Bible, "speaking against God."

> They spoke against God, saying, / "Can God spread a table in the desert? / When he struck the rock, water gushed out, / and streams flowed abundantly. / But can he also give us food? / Can he supply meat for his people?" / When the Lord heard them, he was very angry; / his fire broke out against Jacob, / and his wrath rose against Israel, / for they did not believe in God / or trust in his deliverance. / Yet he gave a command to the skies above / and opened the doors of the heavens; / he rained down manna for the people to eat, / he gave them the grain of heaven.—Ps 78:19-24

Their sorrows came upon them because they did not trust. God was equal to the emergency, but they did not believe it, and their doubt grieved him more than all their other sins.

> And he called the place Massah and Meribah because the Israelites quarreled and because they tested the Lord saying, "Is the Lord among us or not?"—Ex 17:7

Here their questioning is called "testing the Lord." And yet how common is just this sort of questioning among Christians, who little dream what a sin it is!

Let our Lord's own words close our lesson.

> Are not five sparrows sold for two pennies? Yet not one of them is forgotten by God. Indeed, the very hairs of your head are all numbered. Don't be afraid; you are worth more than many sparrows.—Lk 12:6-7

In the face of *such* an assurance, who could doubt? The sparrows, and the hairs of our head, two strikingly insignificant and valueless things! And yet *they* are noticed and cared for. Then surely *we*!

The Sparrow and The Child of God

I am only a tiny sparrow,
    A bird of low degree;
My life is of little value,
    But the dear Lord cares for me.

I have no barn nor storehouse,
   I neither sow nor reap;
God gives me a sparrow's portion,
   But never a seed to keep.

I know there are many sparrows,
   All over the world they are found,
But our heavenly Father knoweth
   When one of us falls to the ground.

Tho' small, we are never forgotten,
   Tho' weak, we are never afraid;
For we know the dear Lord keepeth
   The life of the creatures he made.

I fly through the thickest forest,
   I light on many a spray;
I have no chart nor compass,
   But I never lose my way.

And I fold my wings at twilight
   Wherever I happen to be,
For the Father is always watching,
   And no harm will come to me.

I am only a little sparrow.
   A bird of low degree,
But I know the Father loves me;
   Have you less faith than we?

SIX

Like a Mother

Foundation Text— *As a mother comforts her child, / so will I comfort you; / and you will be comforted over Jerusalem.*
—Is 66:13

We all know how a mother comforts her children, and most of us have tasted the sweetness of this comforting. Notice then, the "as" and "so" in this declaration, and accept the Divine Comforter and the heavenly comfort.

Shout for joy, O heavens; / rejoice, O earth; / burst into song, O mountains! / For the Lord comforts his people / and will have compassion on his afflicted ones.—Is 49:13 (Is 51:3, 12; 52:9)

God is called the "God of all comfort."

Praise be to the God and Father of our Lord Jesus Christ, the Father of compassion and the God of all comfort, who comforts us in all our troubles, so that we can comfort those in any trouble with the comfort we ourselves have received from God.
—2 Cor 1:3-4

The Holy Spirit is called the Comforter.

But the Comforter, which is the Holy Ghost, whom the Father will send in my name, he shall teach you all things, and bring all things to your remembrance, whatsoever I have said unto you.
—Jn 14:26 (KJV)

Christ, when he was leaving his disciples, provided for their comfort when he should be gone.

> And I will pray the Father, and he shall give you another Comforter, that he may abide with you for ever.... I will not leave you comfortless; I will come to you.—Jn 14:16-18 (KJV)

But some will say, if God is like a mother, and comforts as mothers comfort, why is it that they are not comforted?

Have you never seen a little child sitting up stiff in the mother's lap, and refusing to be comforted, in spite of all her coaxing? And do we not often act in very much the same way?

> O Jerusalem, Jerusalem, you who kill the prophets and stone those sent to you, how often I have longed to gather your children together, as a hen gathers her chicks under her wings, but you were not willing.—Mt 23:37

> When I was in distress, I sought the Lord; / at night I stretched out untiring hands / and my soul refused to be comforted.
>
> —Ps 77:2

Even a mother's love and tenderness cannot comfort a child that "refuses to be comforted"; and neither can God's. But no sorrow can be too great for his comfort to reach, if we will only take it.

> Even though I walk / through the valley of the shadow of death, / I will fear no evil, / for you are with me; / your rod and your staff, / they comfort me.—Ps 23:4

> Then maidens will dance and be glad, / young men and old as well. / I will turn their mourning into gladness; / I will give them comfort and joy instead of sorrow.—Jer 31:13

If we will only listen believingly to his loving words: "Daughter be of good comfort"; we shall surely be comforted.

There are many other ways in which God is like a mother, and a comparison of these points will, I trust, open our eyes to see some truths concerning him, which have been hitherto hidden from our gaze.

1. The mother runs when the child cries, and listens to the story of its sorrows and its needs, and relieves them.
And just so God.

Then you will call, and the Lord will answer;
    you will cry for help, and he will say: Here am I.—Is 58:9

The "here am I" of the mother never fails to respond to the child's cry of "Mother, mother, where are you?" And neither does God's (Ps 3:4-5).

To the Lord I cry aloud, / and he answers me from his holy hill. / I lie down and sleep; / I wake again, because the Lord sustains me.—Ps 3:4-5

How alert is the ear of the mother to the feeblest cry of her baby in the night. Let her be sleeping ever so soundly, and she will still hear the tiny cry. And how comforted and quieted the little one is when it realizes its mother's presence and can go to sleep in her care.

When I called, you answered me; / you made me bold and stouthearted.—Ps 138:3 (Ps 77:1)

We are sometimes tempted to think that the Lord does not hear our prayers. But let the mother teach us. Could she possibly let the cry of her child go unheeded? And is the earthly mother more tender of her children, than the heavenly Father is of his?

He provides food for the cattle / and for the young ravens when they call. (Ps 147:9)

Since he hears the cry of the ravens, shall he not hear ours?

Then they cried out to the Lord in their trouble, / and he delivered them from their distress.—Ps 107:6, 13, 19, 28

We are tempted to think that trouble shuts God's ears. In times of prosperity we rejoice to believe he hears us, but when the dark days come, we moan and complain because our prayers do not reach him. Which cry catches the mother's ear the soonest, the cry of joy or the cry of sorrow? There can be but one answer to this. Every mother knows that the happy noises of her children in the nursery pass by often unnoticed, but the slightest cry of pain or trouble reaches her ear at once. And is a mother more alert to the suffering of her children than God?

> Before they call I will answer; / while they are still speaking I will hear.—Is 65:24

Perhaps the child hardly knows why it cries, and cannot tell in any clear way what is the matter with it. But the mother does not refuse, because of this, to listen to its cry. She only seeks instead, all the more, to discover the cause of the discomfort for herself, and to remedy it. And surely, so must God.

> Does he who implanted the ear not hear? / Does he who formed the eye not see?—Ps 94:9

> Surely the arm of the Lord is not too short to save, / nor his ear too dull to hear.—Is 59:1

Let us never grieve him again by doubting that he hears us, however faint and feeble may be our cry. And let us be encouraged to ask as children do, for everything we need, sure that he will always hear, and will always answer (as some one has said), either in *kind* or in kindness.

> Until now you have not asked for anything in my name. Ask and you will receive, and your joy will be complete.—Jn 16:24

2. The mother carries the child in her arms and folds it to her bosom.

> He tends his flock like a shepherd: / He gathers the lambs in his arms / and carries them close to his heart; / he gently leads those that have young.—Is 40:11

Even to your old age and gray hairs / I am he, I am he who will sustain you / I have made you and I will carry you; / I will sustain you and I will rescue you.—Is 46:4

Do we not act sometimes as though we thought we were carrying the Lord, rather than that he was carrying us? And do we not go bowed down under this fancied burden, when we ought to be resting peacefully in his arms? A baby, safe in its mother's arms, will sometimes make little clutches of fright, as though its safety depended upon the strength of its tiny grasp of the mother's neck. But the mother knows how useless these are, and that it is *her* grasp, and not the baby's, that secures its safety. And surely this is true of us in the arms of God.

The eternal God is your refuge, / and underneath are the everlasting arms. / He will drive out your enemy before you, / saying, "Destroy him!"—Dt 33:27

The baby carried in the arms of its mother knows no fear, even though the path may lie through a howling wilderness or through raging enemies. The mother's arms are its impregnable fortress. And the "everlasting arms" of God can be no less.

Like an eagle that stirs up its nest / and hovers over its young, / that spreads its wings to catch them / and carries them on its pinions.—Dt 32:11-12 (Is 63:9)

Even the eagle knows this secret of mother love. When the little eagles are old enough to learn to fly, she stirs up the nest and thrusts them out, that they may be driven to find the use of their wings. But she floats in the air under them, and watches them with eyes of love, and when she sees any little eaglet showing signs of weariness, she flies beneath it and spreads out her great strong mother wings to bear it up until it is rested and ready to fly again. And so the Lord.

All races both of men and animals instinctively recognize the mother's right and duty to bear the burden of the child she has brought into the world. And Moses appealed to this universal instinct when he complained to the Lord concerning the children of Israel.

> Did I conceive all these people? Did I give them birth? Why do you tell me to carry them in my arms, as a nurse carries an infant, to the land you promised on oath to their forefathers?—Nm 11:12

And in rehearsing the wilderness wandering in "the plain over against the Red Sea," he again used the same figure to describe how the Lord had dealt with them.

> . . . and in the desert. There you saw how the Lord your God carried you, as a father carries his son, all the way you went until you reached this place.—Dt 1:31

We cannot make any mistake then, in believing that the Lord carries us in his arms and folds us to his bosom with far more tenderness and watchful care than any mother ever could.

3. The mother wipes away the tears of her little one.

> For the Lamb at the center of the throne will be their shepherd; / he will lead them to springs of living water. / And God will wipe away every tear from their eyes.—Rv 7:17

Where do the little ones run for comfort, but to their mother? They know that no other hand can wipe away their tears as hers can. And have we not often seen children, when they were hurt, holding in the cry until mother came, because they have felt instinctively that nobody but "mother" could sympathize or console?

Shall we not then let our God wipe away the tears from our eyes, and give us "joy for mourning," just as we used to let our mothers do, when we were in their loving care?

> For you, O Lord, have delivered my soul from death, / my eyes from tears, / my feet from stumbling.—Ps 116:8

He will swallow up death forever. / The Sovereign Lord will wipe away the tears / from all faces; / he will remove the disgrace of his people / from all the earth. / The Lord has spoken.
—Is 25:8 (Is 30:19; 6:8-9)

When our Lord was on earth he was very tender of the tears of his people.

When the Lord saw her, his heart went out to her and he said, "Don't cry."—Lk 7:13

Meanwhile, all the people were wailing and mourning for her. "Stop wailing," Jesus said. "She is not dead but asleep."—Lk 8:52

Just as the mother says, "Darling, do not cry," so he says to us, "Weep not." Our tears give him grief.

When Jesus saw her weeping, and the Jews who had come along with her also weeping, he was deeply moved in spirit and troubled.—Jn 11:33

Perhaps we do not remember this enough, and indulge ourselves sometimes in weeping, when our Lord would gladly wipe away our tears. Let us consider this, and see if for his sake, as for our mother's sake, we cannot dry our eyes, and try to bear cheerfully the sorrows he permits to come upon us. Have we never known what it was to restrain our sorrow that we might not grieve a loved one? And shall we not sometimes do this for our Lord?

But be glad and rejoice forever / in what I will create, / for I will create Jerusalem to be a delight / and its people a joy. / I will rejoice over Jerusalem / and take delight in my people; / the sound of weeping and of crying / will be heard in it no more.
—Is 65:18-19

He will wipe every tear from their eyes. There will be no more death or mourning or crying or pain, for the old order of things has passed away.—Rv 21:4

4. The mother watches over her children in sickness, and does all she can to comfort and to heal.

> The Lord will sustain him on his sickbed / and restore him from his bed of illness.—Ps 41:3 (1 Kgs 8:37-39)

Concerning our Lord it was declared that he had borne not our sins only, but our sicknesses as well.

> When evening came, many who were demon possessed were brought to him, and he drove out the spirits with a word and healed all the sick. This was to fulfill what was spoken through the prophet Isaiah: / "He took up our infirmities / and carried our diseases."—Mt 8:16-17

The story of his life on earth was one continual record of his tenderness with sickness, and his power and willingness to heal.

> As soon as they got out of the boat, people recognized Jesus. They ran throughout that whole region and carried the sick on mats to wherever they heard he was. And everywhere he went— into villages, towns or countryside—they placed the sick in the marketplaces. They begged him to let them touch even the edge of his cloak, and all who touched him were healed.
> —Mk 6:54-56 (Mt 4:23)

How literally this bearing of our sicknesses is to be taken is a subject which we cannot consider here. There is a great difference of opinion on the matter. But of this I am sure, that all who trust him will find that the tenderest mother's love and care in sickness is only a faint picture of the love and care that he will bestow.

5. The mother bears with the naughty child as no one else can, and finds excuses for it, and loves it freely through all.

> While Jesus was having dinner at Matthew's house, many tax collectors and "sinners" came and ate with him and his disciples. When the Pharisees saw this, they asked his disciples, "Why does your teacher eat with tax collectors and 'sinners?'"

On hearing this, Jesus said, "It is not the healthy who need a doctor, but the sick. But go and learn what this means: 'I desire mercy, not sacrifice.' For I have not come to call the righteous, but sinners."—Mt 9:10-13

Other people love us when we are good, our mothers love us when we are not. And God is like our mothers.

But God demonstrates his own love for us in this: While we were still sinners, Christ died for us.—Rom 5:8

Here is a trustworthy saying that deserves full acceptance: Christ Jesus came into the world to save sinners—of whom I am the worst.—1 Tm 1:15

Our mothers do not love our *sins,* but they love *us,* even when we are sinners; and they love us enough to try to save us from our sins. And this is like God.

There's a wideness in God's mercy,
    Like the wideness of the sea;
There's a kindness in his justice
    That is more than liberty.

There's no place where earthly sorrows
    Are more felt than up in heaven;
There's no place where earthly failings
    Have such kindly judgment given.

Only mothers can be just to their children, for they alone know their temptations. And only God can be just toward us, for "He alone knows our frame, and remembers that we are dust."

6. The mother will lay down her life for her child. Our Lord laid down his life for us.

I am the good shepherd. The good shepherd lays down his life for the sheep. The hired hand is not the shepherd who owns the sheep. So when he sees the wolf coming, he abandons the sheep and runs away. Then the wolf attacks the flock and scatters it. The man runs away because he is a hired hand and cares nothing for the sheep.

I am the good shepherd; I know my sheep and my sheep know me—just as the Father knows me and I know the Father—and I lay down my life for the sheep.—Jn 10:11-15

This is how we know what love is: Jesus Christ laid down his life for us. And we ought to lay down our lives for our brothers.
—1 Jn 3:16

All nature teaches us this law of the self-sacrifice of motherhood. Even the wild tiger-mother yields to its power. A late writer has said concerning this: "It is a tiger's impulse to resent an injury. Pluck her by the hair, smite her on the flank, she will leap upon and rend you. But to resent an injury is not her strongest impulse. Watch those impotent kitten creatures playing with her. They are so weak, a careless movement of her giant paw would destroy them; but she makes no careless movement. They have caused her a hundredfold the pain your blow produced; yet she does not render evil for evil. These puny mites of helpless impotence she strokes, with love's light in her eyes; she licks the shapeless forms of her tormentors, and, as they plunge at her, each groan of her anguish is transformed by love into a whinney of delight. She moves her massive head in a way which shows that he, who bade you turn the other cheek, created her. When strong enough to rise, the terrible creature goes forth to sacrifice herself for her own. She will starve that they may thrive. She is terrible for her little ones, as Christ was terrible for his. He who made her, taught her the secret of motherhood."

The little Bantam hen has learned the same secret, and will spread her tiny wings and rush to her death, if her little chicks are in danger.

In all ranges of being, the beautiful law of motherhood leads to the grandeur of an utter self-sacrifice. And he who conceived and created motherhood, cannot himself do less than the mothers he has made.

For Christ's love compels us, because we are convinced that one died for all, and therefore all died. And he died for all, that those who live should no longer live for themselves but for him who died for them and was raised again.

—2 Cor 5:14-15 (Rom 5:6; 1 Thes 5:9-10)

"When the polar bear lays down her life for the cub that cannot live without her; when the leopard gives herself to death in defence of her impotent whelp; the Artic Circle and the Libyan zone unite in protestation that the spirit of Nature is the spirit of Christ."

7. The mother holds the hand of her child to lead it in the right path, and lifts it over the rough places, that it may not stumble.

For he will command his angels concerning you / to guard you in all your ways; / they will lift you up in their hands, / so that you will not strike your foot against a stone.—Ps 91:11-12

To him who is able to keep you from falling and to present you before his glorious presence without fault and with great joy.

—Jude 24 (1 Sm 2:9; Prv 2:26)

It is the mother who holds the child, not the child the mother. It is the mother who watches the path, and lifts the baby feet over the stones and snares that obstruct the way. The responsibility is all hers. The child has only to abandon itself to her leading, and trust her fully. And our God knows the way we take, and will direct all our steps, if we but commit ourselves to his care.

He will not let your foot slip— / he who watches over you will not slumber;—Ps 121:3

My eyes are ever on the Lord, / for only he will release my feet from the snare.—Ps 25:15

He lifted me out of the slimy pit, / out of the mud and mire; / he set my feet on a rock / and gave me a firm place to stand.—Ps 40:2

You give me your shield of victory, / and your right hand sustains me; / you stoop down to make me great. / You broaden the path beneath me, / so that my ankles do not turn.

—Ps 18:35-36 (Ps 17:5)

No matter how much the child may resist the mother's leading, or wander from her loving clasp, still she is always ready again to take hold of its hand and lead it.

If I rise on the wings of the dawn, / if I settle on the far side of the sea, / even there your hand will guide me, / your right hand will hold me fast.—Ps 139:9-10 (Is 41:13)

8. The mother is always ready to feed her hungry child, and would starve herself before she would suffer the child to starve.

The eyes of all look to you, / and you give them their food at the proper time. / You open your hand / and satisfy the desires of every living thing.—Ps 145:15-16

Blessed are those who hunger and thirst for righteousness, / for they will be filled.—Mt 5:6 (Ps 107:9)

It is not always the food the child asks for, that the wise mother gives. Sometimes such food would be fatal to its health. But it is always the food that is best for it, up to the mother's light and ability to procure. And we may be perfectly sure that our God always gives us that which is best, whether it is what we ask for or not. Therefore we must be satisfied.

My soul will be satisfied as with the richest of foods; / with singing lips my mouth will praise you.—Ps 63:5

Which of you fathers, if your son asks for a fish, will give him a snake instead? Or if he asks for an egg, will give him a scorpion? If you then, though you are evil, know how to give good gifts to your children, how much more will your Father in heaven give the Holy Spirit to those who ask him!—Lk 11:11-13

What our Father gives may *look* to us like a "snake" or a "scorpion," but, since he gives it, we may be sure it cannot be anything but just the best thing for us. For if parents "know how" to give good gifts how "much more" must he? (Mt 6:25-26, 33)

The child does not have to supply or prepare its own food; this is the mother's business. And all the child has to do is to eat and live, without care and without cost (Mt 6:25-26, 33; Is 55:1-2).

9. The mother takes pleasure in her child, and loves to dress it beautifully and to keep it clean.

> I delight greatly in the Lord; / my soul rejoices in my God. / For he has clothed me with garments of salvation / and arrayed me in a robe of righteousness, / as a bridegroom adorns his head like a priest, / and as a bride adorns herself with her jewels.
> —Is 61:10 (Ps 149:4)

What joy in the world is equal to the joy of a mother in her child! And what employment is sweeter to her than to prepare dainty garments for its adorning.

And yet it is hard for the children themselves to believe this. They do not know the mother's heart, and they cannot enter into her joy in them.

And it is the same with us toward our God. We cannot believe that he *can* take pleasure in such poor miserable creatures as we are. We know we delight in him, but it seems impossible that he should delight in us. And yet, in spite of all the child's ignorance of it, the mother does rejoice in her little ones; and in spite of our doubts and fears God does rejoice in us.

> The Lord delights in those who fear him, / who put their hope in his unfailing love. —Ps 147:11

Can not we therefore, who understand something of the mother's heart towards her children, understand also something of the heart of God towards us?

> I gave you my solemn oath and entered into a covenant with you, declares the Sovereign Lord, and you became mine.

I bathed you with water and washed the blood from you and put ointments on you. I clothed you with an embroidered dress and put leather sandals on you. I dressed you in fine linen and covered you with costly garments. I adorned you with jewelry: I put bracelets on your arms and a necklace around your neck, and I put a ring on your nose, earrings on your ears and a beautiful crown on your head. So you were adorned with gold and silver; your clothes were of fine linen and costly fabric and embroidered cloth. Your food was fine flour, honey and olive oil. You became very beautiful and rose to be a queen. And your fame spread among the nations on account of your beauty, because the splendor I had given you made your beauty perfect, declares the Sovereign Lord.—Ez 16:8-14 (Ps 45:13-14)

The child does not make its own clothes, but leaves them all for the mother.

And why do you worry about clothes? See how the lilies of the field grow. They do not labor or spin. Yet I tell you that not even Solomon in all his splendor was dressed like one of these. If that is how God clothes the grass of the field, which is here today and tomorrow is thrown into the fire, will he not much more clothe you, O you of little faith?—Mt 6:28-30

It would grieve the mother to see her little one anxious and troubled about its clothing; and it grieves our God to see us. Moreover, all our efforts to clothe ourselves are grievous failures, just as the child's would be.

What are you doing, O devastated one? / Why dress yourself in scarlet / and put on jewels of gold? / Why shade your eyes with paint? / You adorn yourself in vain. / Your lovers despise you; / they seek your life.—Jer 4:30

Only the Lord can clothe us; and he only can make us clean.

"Come now, let us reason together,"/ says the Lord. / "Though your sins are like scarlet, / they shall be as white as snow; / though they are red as crimson, / they shall be like wool."
—Is 1:18 (1 Jn 1:7, 9)

10. The mother feels the hurts and sufferings of her child as though they were her own.

> In all their distress he too was distressed, / and the angel of his presence saved them. / In his love and mercy he redeemed them; / he lifted them up and carried them / all the days of old. —Is 63:9

Even though the affliction may be the result of sin, still the mother grieves over it and longs to help it. Strangers may say "It serves you right," but no good mother ever could.

> For we do not have a high priest who is unable to sympathize with our weaknesses, but we have one who has been tempted in every way, just as we are—yet was without sin. —Heb 4:15

> Whoever touches you touches the apple of his eye. —Zech 2:8

11. The mother cannot forget or forsake her child. And yet even this *may* be possible with a human mother, but with God never!

> But Zion said, "The Lord has forsaken me, / the Lord has forgotten me." / "Can a mother forget the baby at her breast / and have no compassion on the child she has borne? / Though she may forget, / I will not forget you! / See, I have engraved you on the palms of my hands; / your walls are ever before me.
> —Is 49:14-16

> Why do you say, O Jacob, / and complain, O Israel / "My way is hidden from the Lord; / my cause is disregarded by my God?" / Do you not know? / Have you not heard? / The Lord is the everlasting God, / the Creator of the ends of the earth. / He will not grow tired or weary, / and his understanding no one can fathom. / He gives strength to the weary / and increases the power of the weak. —Is 40:27-29

Christians sometimes talk as though God had forsaken them; but this is impossible, for he has said, "Never will I leave you; never will I forsake you." (Heb 13:5-6; Dt 31:6-8)

The child in delirium thinks its mother has forsaken it,

although all the time she is close beside it. And we, in the delirium of our doubts and fears, think as falsely, that God has forsaken us.

> For the sake of his great name the Lord will not reject his people, because the Lord was pleased to make you his own.
> —1 Sm 12:22 (1 Kgs 6:13; Josh 1:5)

12. The mother stays beside her child when it is in danger, even though all others may abandon it.

> I am the good shepherd. The good shepherd lays down his life for the sheep. The hired hand is not the shepherd who owns the sheep. So when he sees the wolf coming, he abandons the sheep and runs away. Then the wolf attacks the flock and scatters it. The man runs away because he is a hired hand and cares nothing for the sheep.—Jn 10:11-13

A hired nurse, no matter how much she is paid, may flee in a moment of danger, and leave her charge to its fate. But danger only makes the mother keep closer to her helpless little one. The mother-hen, who generally flies at the first approach of danger, will stand as firm and dauntless as a lion, if she has her little chickens to guard.

Have we ever dared to think of our Lord as though he were a "hired hand" who fled when danger approached?

Have we not even sometimes been more ready to trust earthly hirelings, than to trust him?

> The Lord is a refuge for the oppressed, / a stronghold in times of trouble.—Ps 9:9

> For in the day of trouble / he will keep me safe in his dwelling; / he will hide me in the shelter of his tabernacle / and set me high upon a rock.—Ps 27:5

13. If the child is lost, the mother leaves all else to seek it, and never gives up "till she finds it."

Then Jesus told them this parable: "Suppose one of you has a hundred sheep and loses one of them. Does he not leave the ninety-nine in the open country and go after the lost sheep until he finds it? And when he finds it, he joyfully puts it on his shoulders and goes home. Then he calls his friends and neighbors together and says, 'Rejoice with me'; I have found my lost sheep.' I tell you that in the same way there is more rejoicing in heaven over one sinner who repents than over ninety-nine righteous persons who do not need to repent.—Lk 15:3-10 (Mt 18:11-14; 34:11-12)

What, then, is the summing up of the whole matter? Simply this: If God is only as good as the mothers he has made, where can there be any room left for a thought of care or of fear? And if he is as much truer to the ideal of motherhood than an earthly mother can be, as his infiniteness is above hers, then what oceans and continents of bliss are ours for the taking!
Shall we not take it?

Learn of this mother to be no more beguiled,
    For, mindful of the mother heart which I have given;
She in my goodness hath abiding faith;
    And whatso'er of Me another saith,
Although the words may *seem* to come from heaven;
    She ponders well, and tries it by the test,
Of that which in her own heart she finds best.

SEVEN

Like Little Children

Foundation Text— *People were also bringing babies to Jesus to have him touch them. When the disciples saw this, they rebuked them. But Jesus called the children to him and said, "Let the little children come to me, and do not hinder them, for the kingdom of God belongs to such as these. I tell you the truth, anyone who will not receive the kingdom of God like a little child will never enter it."* —Lk 18:15-17

Notice that in verse fifteen the word used to describe the little children whom our Lord here takes as patterns for us, is "babies"; and in verse sixteen, he says concerning them, "the kingdom of God belongs to such as these."

At that time Jesus, full of joy through the Holy Spirit, said, "I praise you, Father, Lord of heaven and earth, because you have hidden these things from the wise and learned, and revealed them to little children. Yes, Father, for this was your good pleasure."
—Lk 10:21

At that time the disciples came to Jesus and asked, "Who is the greatest in the kingdom of heaven?"

He called a little child and had him stand among them. And he said: "I tell you the truth, unless you change and become like little children, you will never enter the kingdom of heaven. Therefore, whoever humbles himself like this child is the greatest in the kingdom of heaven."—Mt 18:1-4

It is plainly therefore *little* children, "babies," who are to be our patterns; not grown-up children, nor half-grown ones; not precocious children, nor children who have old heads on young shoulders. But real, honest, downright *little* children, who have all the characteristics of what George Macdonald calls "childness," which means the guileless, impulsive, tender, trustful, self-forgetting, uncareful spirit of a *little* child.

It is of vital importance then, that we should get a true idea of what it means to be a little child, and of the characteristics of ideal childhood, in order that we may know what must be our characteristics, if we would become "as little children."

1. A little child takes no anxious thought for the supply of its needs, but leaves all the care of providing to its parents. And we likewise must take no anxious thought for the supply of our needs; but must leave all the care of providing to our heavenly Father.

> Therefore I tell you, do not worry about your life, what you will eat or drink; or about your body, what you will wear. Is not life more important than food, and the body more important than clothes? Look at the birds of the air; they do not sow or reap or store away in barns, and yet your heavenly Father feeds them. Are you not much more valuable than they?—Mt 6:25-26
>
> Cast all your anxiety on him because he cares for you.
> —1 Pt 5:7 (Mt 6:31-33)

2. A little child lives in the present moment, and leaves the planning of its future to the mother's care.

We also must live in the present moment and leave our future to God.

> Therefore do not worry about tomorrow, for tomorrow will worry about itself. Each day has enough trouble of its own.
> —Mt 6:34

3. A little child asks for everything it wants, without ceremony, and in a joyous confidence of being heard and answered.

We also must ask in unceremonious childlike confidence for everything we want, sure of being heard and answered, according to God's divine wisdom.

Do not be anxious about anything, but in everything, by prayer and petition, with thanksgiving, present your requests to God.
—Phil 4:6

If you remain in me and my words remain in you, ask whatever you wish, and it will be given you.—Jn 15:7

Therefore I tell you, whatever you ask for in prayer, believe that you have received it, and it will be yours.—Mk 11:24 (Mt 7:7-11)

4. The little child runs to its mother for comfort in all its troubles.
We also must go to our Lord for comfort in all our troubles.

For this is what the Lord says, / "I will extend peace to her like a river, / and the wealth of nations like a flooding stream; / you will nurse and be carried on her arm / and dandled on her knees. / As a mother comforts her child, / so will I comfort you; / and you will be comforted over Jerusalem."—Is 66:12-13 (2 Cor 1:3-4)

5. The little child looks to its father and mother for deliverance from all its enemies.
And likewise we must look to our God for deliverance from ours.

For he will deliver the needy who cry out,
    the afflicted who have no one to help.
        —Ps 72:12 (Ps 22:4-5; 34:6; 107:6)

6. A little child rests in the mother's arms when it is weary.
And likewise we must rest our weary souls in the arms of our God.

Come to me, all you who are weary and burdened, and I will give you rest.—Mt 11:28 (Is 32:18)

This is what the Sovereign Lord, the Holy One of Israel, says:

"In repentance and rest is your salvation, / in quietness and trust is your strength.—Is 30:15

7. The little child asks questions about everything it wants to know, and believes all that its mother says, without question or doubt.

And likewise we must ask our Lord about everything in which we lack wisdom, and must believe all that he says with implicit confidence.

If any of you lacks wisdom, he should ask God, who gives generously to all without finding fault, and it will be given to him. But when he asks, he must believe and not doubt, because he who doubts is like a wave of the sea, blown and tossed by the wind. That man should not think he will receive anything from the Lord; he is a double-minded man, unstable in all he does.—Jas 1:5-7

But the Counselor, the Holy Spirit, whom the Father will send in my name, will teach you all things and will remind you of everything I have said to you.—Jn 14:26 (Prv 2:3-6)

8. The little child expects its father and mother to fight all its battles, and is always confident that they can conquer.

And likewise we must expect our Lord to fight all our battles, and must be confident in his certain victory.

Moses answered the people, "Do not be afraid. Stand firm and you will see the deliverance the Lord will bring you today. The Egyptians you see today you will never see again. The Lord will fight for you; you need only to be still."
—Ex 14:13-14 (Rom 12:19; Ps 60:12; Dt 20:1-4; Ex 15:1-3)

9. The little child takes refuge in its mother's arms when an enemy approaches, and is afraid of nothing in her presence.

And likewise we must make the Lord our refuge, and must fear nothing in his presence.

The eternal God is your refuge, / and underneath are the everlasting arms. / He will drive out your enemy before you, / saying, "Destroy him!"—Dt 33:27

The Lord is my light and my salvation— / whom shall I fear? / The Lord is the stronghold of my life— / of whom shall I be afraid? / When evil men advance against me / to devour my flesh, / when my enemies and my foes attack me, / they will stumble and fall. / Though an army besiege me, / my heart will not fear; / though war break out against me, / even then will I be confident.
—Ps 27:1-3 (Ps 46:1-3; Ps 91:2-10; Ps 9:9-10)

10. The little child believes its parents can do everything and that nothing is too hard for them.

And we must believe that all things are possible to our Father in heaven, and that nothing can thwart his blessed will.

Then the disciples came to Jesus in private and asked, "Why couldn't we drive it out?"

He replied, "Because you have so little faith. I tell you the truth, if you have faith as small as a mustard seed, you can say to this mountain, 'Move from here to there' and it will move. Nothing will be impossible for you."
—Mt 17:19-20 (Rom 4:20-21; Mk 9:23; Mt 9:28-29)

11. The little child is never surprised at the greatness of any gift that its parents may offer, nor ever hesitates from a foolish mistrust, to accept the most lavish presents.

And likewise we must not be hindered by a foolish mistrust from accepting eagerly and gladly the lavish gifts which our Lord is continually seeking to bestow upon us.

I am the Lord your God, / who brought you up out of Egypt. / Open wide your mouth and I will fill it.—Ps 81:10

For if, by the trespass of the one man, death reigned through that one man, how much more will those who receive God's abundant provision of grace and of the gift of righteousness reign in life through the one man, Jesus Christ.
—Rom 5:17 (1 Cor 2:9-10; Eph 3:20-21)

12. The little child never doubts the love and care of its mother, and would be surprised beyond measure should there be any lack.

And we must never doubt the love and care of our Lord, nor be surprised at his tender watchfulness of all our needs.

> If that is how God clothes the grass of the field, which is here today and tomorrow is thrown into the fire, will he not much more clothe you, O you of little faith?
> —Mt 6:30 (Mk 4:35-40; Ps 78:19-24; Mt 16:8-10; Jn 14:1-3)

13. The little child is content with the arrangements its mother makes for it, and asks no questions.

And we likewise must be content with our Lord's arrangements for us, and ask no questions, nor murmur at the dispensations he may permit.

> But who are you, O man, to talk back to God? "Shall what is formed say to him who formed it, 'Why did you make me like this?'"—Rom 9:20

> But godliness with contentment is great gain. For we brought nothing into the world, and we can take nothing out of it. But if we have food and clothing, we will be content with that.
> —1 Tm 6:6-8 (Ex 17:1-3, 7; 1 Cor 10:10-11; Phil 4:11-12; Heb 13:5)

14. Little children grow as the flowers grow, without taking any thought about their growing.

And we must consider the lilies how they grow and grow like them, without anxiety or strain.

> Who of you by worrying can add a single hour to his life?
> And why do you worry about clothes? See how the lilies of the field grow. They do not labor or spin. Yet I tell you that not even Solomon in all his splendor was dressed like one of these.
> —Mt 6:27-29 (Hos 14:5-6; Ps 92:12-14; Jer 17:7-8; 1 Pt 2:2)

15. The little child comes with boldness into its mother's presence, and never doubts her loving welcome.

And likewise we also must come with boldness into the

presence of our Lord, without a question or doubt of his loving welcome.

> And so we know and rely on the love God has for us.
> God is love. Whoever lives in love lives in God, and God in him. Love is made complete among us so that we will have confidence on the day of judgment, because in this world we are like him. There is no fear in love. But perfect love drives out fear, because fear has to do with punishment. The man who fears is not made perfect in love.
> —1 Jn 4:16-18 (Heb 10:19-23; Eph 3:12; Heb 4:15-16; 13:6)

16. The little child boasts about its parents, and wants to tell everyone of their goodness.

And we must make our boast in the Lord, and tell of his wonderful goodness, wherever we can.

> I will extol the Lord at all times; / his praise will always be on my lips. / My soul will boast in the Lord; / let the afflicted hear and rejoice. / Glorify the Lord with me; / let us exalt his name together.—Ps 34:1-3

> In God we make our boast all day long, / and we will praise your name forever.—Ps 44:8 (Ps 33:1-3; Mk 5:19-20; Is 63:7)

17. Little children are punished when they do wrong, and are subdued and softened by the punishment, and kiss the hand that smites.

And likewise the Lord chastises us when we are naughty, and we must accept our chastisements with thankful submission, letting them work in our spirits the purposed blessing.

> Those whom I love I rebuke and discipline. So be earnest, and repent.—Rv 3:19

> Blessed is the man whom God corrects; / so do not despise the discipline of the Almighty.—Jb 5:17-18

> And you have forgotten that word of encouragement that addresses you as sons: "My son, do not make light of the Lord's

discipline, / and do not lose heart when he rebukes you, / because the Lord disciplines those he loves, / and he punishes everyone he accepts as a son.—Heb 12:5-6 (Ps 94:12; Heb 12:7-11)

18. Little children have teachable spirits, and are eager to learn.

We also must have teachable spirits, and must be eager to be taught by God.

A wise son heeds his father's instruction, / but a mocker does not listen to rebuke.—Prv 13:1

How sweet are your promises to my taste, / sweeter than honey to my mouth! / I gain understanding from your precepts; / therefore I hate every wrong path.
—Ps 119:103-104 (Jn 16:12-13 Prv 12:1; Ps 119:97-102; Jn 14:26)

19. The little child has a ready foot to run the mother's errands.

We also must have ready feet to run on our Father's business.

I run in the path of your commands, / for you have set my heart free.—Ps 119:32 (Ps 119:59-60)

20. Little children have obedient spirits, and do what their parents desire, and not what they may think best themselves.

And we likewise must have obedient spirits to do God's will, and not our own, no matter how much better our own plans may seem to us.

But I gave them this command: Obey me, and I will be your God and you will be my people. Walk in all the ways I command you, that it may go well with you. But they did not listen or pay attention; instead, they followed the stubborn inclinations of their evil hearts. They went backward and not forward.
—Jer 7:23-24

Not everyone who says to me, "Lord, Lord," will enter the kingdom of heaven, but only he who does the will of my Father who is in heaven.
—Mt 7:21 (1 Sm 15:22-23; Lk 6:46-49; 1 Pt 1:14-16)

21. Little children instinctively realize the fact that they have nothing to do but to obey their parents, and leave all else to them.

And likewise we also must intelligently realize the blessed fact that we have nothing to do but to obey our Lord and to leave all else to his care.

But seek first his kingdom and his righteousness, and all these things will be given to you as well.—Mt 6:33 (Eccl 12:13)

Christ was the pattern of this divine childhood.

For to us a child is born, / to us a son is given, / and the government will be on his shoulders. / And he will be called / Wonderful Counselor, Mighty God, / Everlasting Father, Prince of Peace.—Is 9:6

He did nothing of himself.

Jesus gave them this answer: "I tell you the truth, the Son can do nothing by himself; he can do only what he sees his Father doing, because whatever the Father does the Son also does.—Jn 5:19

He said nothing of himself.

So Jesus said, "When you have lifted up the Son of Man, then you will know who I am and that I do nothing on my own but speak just what the Father has taught me.—Jn 8:28 (Jn 12:48-50)

He walked in childlike obedience.

Then he went down to Nazareth with them and was obedient to them. But his mother treasured all these things in her heart.
—Lk 2:51 (Jn 4:34; 6:38)

He referred everything to his Father.

Then Jesus cried out, "When a man believes in me, he does not believe in me only, but in the one who sent me.—Jn 12:44-45

Philip said, "Lord, show us the Father and that will be enough for us."

Jesus answered: "Don't you know me, Philip, even after I have been among you such a long time? Anyone who has seen me has seen the Father. How can you say, 'Show us the Father?'
—Jn 14:8-9 (Jn 8:42)

Since Christ is our example, we must walk as he walked, with the spirit and ways of childhood.

To this you were called, because Christ suffered for you, leaving you an example, that you should follow in his steps.—1 Pt 2:21

Whoever claims to live in him must walk as Jesus did.—1 Jn 2:6

As A Little Child

"unless you change and become like little children,
you will never enter the kingdom of heaven." —Mt 18:3b

"As a little child, as a little child!
   Then how can I enter in?
I am scarred, and hardened, and soul-defiled,
   With traces of sorrow and sin.
Can I turn backward the tide of years
   And wake my dead youth at my will?"
"Nay, but thou canst, with thy grief and thy fears,
   Creep into my arms and be still."

I know that the lambs in the heavenly fold
   Are sheltered and kept in thy heart;
But I, I am old, and the gray from the gold
   Has bidden all brightness depart.
The gladness of youth, the faith and the truth,
   Lie withered or shrouded in dust."
"Thou'rt emptied at length of thy treacherous strength;
   Creep into my arms now, and trust."

Is it true? can I share with the little ones there
   A child's happy rest on Thy breast?"
"Aye, the tenderest care will answer thy prayer,
   My love is for thee as the rest.

It will quiet thy fears, will wipe away tears,
    Thy murmurs shall soften to psalms,
Thy sorrows shall seem but a feverish dream,
    In the rest, in the rest in my arms.

"Thus tenderly held, the heart that rebelled,
    Shall cling to my hand, though it smite;
Shall find in my rod the love of its God,
    My statutes its songs in the night.
And whiter than snow shall the stained life grow,
    'Neath the touch of a love undefiled,
And the throngs of forgiven at the portals of heaven,
    Shall welcome one more little child."

"Therefore, whoever humbles himself like this child is the
greatest in the kingdom of heaven." —Mt 18:4

EIGHT

Fact, Faith, Feeling

THERE IS IN ALL THINGS a divine order, and a human order, and very frequently these two are opposed to one another.

In the three F's we are considering, this is strikingly the case. God's order reads thus;

1. Fact.
2. Faith.
3. Feeling.

In man's order this is reversed;

1. Feeling.
2. Faith.
3. Fact.

That is; in the divine order God gives us first the facts of his salvation; then we believe these facts; and then as a consequence, we have the feelings suitable to the facts believed.

But man reverses this order, and says, "I must have the feeling first, and then I can believe in that feeling, and thus I shall get hold of the facts."

Of course this is absurd; but it is a very common temptation, and is the cause of most of the pitiful uncertainty and doubt that characterizes so much of the experiences of Christians.

And this is the testimony: God has given us eternal life, and this life is his Son. He who has the Son has life; he who does not have the Son of God does not have life. I write these things to you who believe in the name of the Son of God so that you may know that you have eternal life.—1 Jn 5:11-13

Here we have an illustration of the divine order.

First we have the record, that "God has given us eternal life," and that this life is in his Son; and further, that "He who has the Son has life." Then we are told that if we believe these facts, we shall "know" that we have the eternal life spoken of.

> Anyone who believes in the Son of God has this testimony in his heart. Anyone who does not believe God has made him out to be a liar; because he has not believed the testimony God has given about his Son.—1 Jn 5:10

Notice it is he who believes that has the "testimony," not he that doubts. Most people read this passage as though it said "he that doubts shall have the testimony, and then he can believe." They put the testimony, the fact, first and the believing second, but God's order is, first believe, and then have the testimony. And we can never reverse this order; for it is in the very nature of things, as well as in the Book. In all earthly things we require the fact before the feeling. No man starts on a journey at haphazard, and then shuts his eyes to *feel* whether or not he is going the right way. No man sits down to *feel* whether he has money in the bank with which to pay his debts. "Give us the facts" is always our cry in earthly things. But when it comes to spiritual things, we reverse this order entirely, and instead of asking "What is the fact?" we say plaintively, "How do I feel?"

> By the rivers of Babylon we sat and wept / when we remembered Zion. / There on the poplars / we hung our harps, / for there our captors asked us for songs, / our tormentors demanded songs of joy; / they said, "Sing us one of the songs of Zion!" / How can we sing the songs of the Lord / while in a foreign land?—Ps 137:1-4

No one can sing a song of rejoicing unless the cause for rejoicing has first been ascertained to be a fact. The Israelites did not say, "We will feel happy and sing songs, and then we shall be in our own land." We cannot imagine anyone in his senses doing such a silly thing. And yet many a child of God says something every nearly akin to this. "If I could only *feel* happy, then I could believe that God is my Father and that He loves me." We can only know that God loves us by his *saying* so, not by our *feeling* so. We can only know that our earthly friends love us from their own words. We believe them when they tell us that they love us, and then we feel happy because we believe it.

> When the Lord brought back the captives to Zion, / we were like men who dreamed. / Our mouths were filled with laughter, / our tongues with songs of joy. / Then it was said among the nations, / "The Lord has done great things for them." / The Lord has done great things for us, / and we are filled with joy.—Ps 126:1-3

When their captivity was ended, the Israelites rejoiced without any effort. They *could not* sing songs of joy in the strange land, but as soon as they were at home again, their tongues were filled with singing. And we are like them; we *cannot* rejoice until we also know that our captivity has been ended; but when we do know it, our mouths, like theirs, are filled with laughter and our tongues with singing, without any effort.

> "I will extend peace to her like a river, / and the wealth of nations like a flooding stream; / you will nurse and be carried on her arm / and dandled on her knees. / As a mother comforts her child, / so will I comfort you; / and you will be comforted over Jerusalem." / When you see this, your heart will rejoice / and you will flourish like grass; / the hand of the Lord will be made known to his servants, / but his fury will be shown to his foes.
> —Is 66:12-14 (Ps 98:1-6)

"When you see this, your heart will rejoice." We need to "see" our blessings before we can rejoice over them. The Israelites could see their blessings with their outward eyes, for they were visible and tangible things. But we must see ours with our inward eyes, for they are invisible and spiritual. Our knowledge concerning them can only come by *faith,* while theirs came by *sight.* But faith is inward seeing. To believe a thing on sufficient authority is as real as seeing it.

> Therefore, since we have been justified through faith, we have peace with God through our Lord Jesus Christ, through whom we have gained access by faith into this grace in which we now stand. And we rejoice in the hope of the glory of God.
> —Rom 5:1-2

> Praise be to the God and Father of our Lord Jesus Christ! In his great mercy he has given us new birth into a living hope through the resurrection of Jesus Christ from the dead, and into an inheritance that can never perish, spoil or fade—kept in heaven for you, who through faith are shielded by God's power until the coming of the salvation that is ready to be revealed in the last time. In this you greatly rejoice, though now for a little while you may have had to suffer grief in all kinds of trials.
> —1 Pt 1:3-6 (Ps 33:21; Ps 89:15-18)

Our feelings of joy come from our believing joyful facts. The facts do not exist because we are joyful, but we are joyful, on account of the existence of the facts.

Spiritual facts can only be known by believing God's witness concerning them.

> We accept man's testimony, but God's testimony is greater because it is the testimony of God, which he has given about his Son.—1 Jn 5:9

If we are willing to accept man's testimony concerning the facts which come within the range of man's knowledge (and of course we do this every moment), we surely ought to be willing to receive "God's testimony" concerning the facts that come within the range of his knowledge. We could not have a moment's peace in our life among men, if we refused to receive their "testimony," and we can never have a moment's peace in our life with God as long as we refuse to receive his witness. Suppose we should meet every statement of our fellow men with the assertion that we could not believe what they said until we had sat down and looked inside to see whether we *felt* it was true! And yet this is just the way many treat God!

> The one who comes from above is above all; the one who is from the earth belongs to the earth, and speaks as one from the earth. The one who comes from heaven is above all. He testifies to what he has seen and heard, but no one accepts his testimony. The man who has accepted it has certified that God is truthful.
>
> —Jn 3:31-33

What *we* could not know because we are "from the earth," Christ knew because he came from heaven; and what he has seen and heard, he has testified to us. We can only know of heavenly things therefore by believing his words.

> Then Jesus cried out, "When a man believes in me, he does not believe in me only, but in the one who sent me. When he looks at me, he sees the one who sent me. I have come into the world as a light, so that no one who believes in me should stay in darkness.
>
> As for the person who hears my words but does not keep them, I do not judge him. For I did not come to judge the world, but to save it. There is a judge for the one who rejects me and does not accept my words; that very word which I spoke will condemn him at the last day. For I did not speak of my own accord, but the Father who sent me commanded me what to say and how to say it. I know that his command leads to eternal life. So whatever I say is just what the Father has told me to say."—Jn 12:44-50

We see, therefore, that in all our relations with God, we must follow his divine order of, fact first, faith second, and feeling last, if we would be right.

Let us then trace this divine order in regard to some of the most vital points of Christian experience.

1. That God loves us.

The fact

> For God so loved the world that he gave his one and only Son, that whoever believes in him shall not perish but have eternal life.—Jn 3:16

This is love: not that we loved God, but that he loved us and sent his Son as an atoning sacrifice for our sins.—1 Jn 4:10

The faith

And so we know and rely on the love God has for us.
God is love. Whoever lives in love lives in God, and God in him.—1 Jn 4:16

The feeling

And hope does not disappoint us, because God has poured out his love into our hearts by the Holy Spirit, whom he has given us.—Rom 5:5

The great torment of many Christian hearts is that they do not *feel* as if God loved them or they loved him. The trouble is that they are beginning at the wrong end, the end of feeling instead of the end of faith. We never *can* love him, until we first know that he loves us.

We love because he first loved us.—1 Jn 4:19

We are all the time reversing this, and thinking that he will love us if we will first love him. But it is a hopeless attempt; love must begin with God, and we can never originate it ourselves.

2. The forgiveness of sins.

The fact

Therefore, my brothers, I want you to know that through Jesus the forgiveness of sins is proclaimed to you.—Acts 13:38

The faith

Through him everyone who believes is justified from everything you could not be justified from by the law of Moses.—Acts 13:39

The feeling

Therefore, since we have been justified through faith, we have peace with God through our Lord Jesus Christ, through whom we have gained access by faith into the grace in which we now stand. And we rejoice in the hope of the glory of God.

—Rom 5:1-2

The fact is preached to us. We believe the word preached. And as a result we have peace.

But some may ask, Is the fact true until we believe it? Are my sins forgiven before I believe that they are? Certainly they are. In the heart of God there is always forgiveness, like the mother, whose forgiveness always awaits the sin of her child. But this forgiveness cannot reach us until, we believe in it. Our faith does not induce God to forgive us; it is not in any sense the cause of our forgiveness. Faith is only the hand by which we lay hold experimentally of the forgiveness that is already ours in Christ.

I write to you, dear children, / because your sins have been forgiven on account of his name.—1 Jn 2:12

Then he opened their minds so they could understand the Scriptures. He told them, "This is what is written: The Christ will suffer and rise from the dead on the third day, and repentance and forgiveness of sins will be preached in his name to all nations, beginning at Jerusalem.—Lk 24:45-47 (2 Cor 5:18-21)

God *is* reconciled to us; he *has* forgiven us; our sins do not separate him from us, but only us from him. We are not reconciled to him, it may be, but he is always reconciled to us.

Therefore our forgiveness is a fact in the mind and heart of God towards us, before we believe it; and we do not make it true by believing it, but we believe it because it is true. And peace is the result of the believing, not the believing the result of the peace.

3. Eternal life.

The fact

And this is the testimony: God has given us eternal life, and this life is in his Son.—1 Jn 5:11

The faith

Just as Moses lifted up the snake in the desert, so the Son of Man must be lifted up, that everyone who believes in him may have eternal life. —Jn 3:14-15

The feeling

Though you have not seen him, you love him; and even though you do not see him now, you believe in him and are filled with an inexpressible and glorious joy, for you are receiving the goal of your faith, the salvation of your souls. —1 Pt 1:8-9

God has given us eternal life in Christ. Christ is, as it were, a great reservoir of life, out of whom each one of us may take by faith all of life that we need.

In him was life, and that life was the light of men.... Yet to all who received him, to those who believed in his name, he gave the right to become children of God. —Jn 1:4, 12 (1 Jn 1:1-2; Rom 6:23)

We do not have to create this life, nor earn it, nor buy it. We can only receive it as a gift, just as we received our human life. And our receiving is by faith; or in other words by believing that it *has been* given, and that we *have* it.

For my Father's will is that everyone who looks to the Son and believes in him shall have eternal life, and I will raise him up at the last day. —Jn 6:40

Jesus said to her, "I am the resurrection and the life. He who believes in me will live, even though he dies; and whoever lives and believes in me will never die. Do you believe this?"

—Jn 11:25-26

4. The gift of the Holy Spirit.

The fact

And I will ask the Father, and he will give you another Counselor to be with you forever—the Spirit of truth. The world cannot accept him, because it neither sees him nor knows him. But you know him, for he lives with you and will be in you. —Jn 14:16-17

God has raised this Jesus to life, and we are all witnesses of the fact. Exalted to the right hand of God, he has received from the Father the promised Holy Spirit and has poured out what you now see and hear.—Acts 2:32-33

The faith

On the last and greatest day of the Feast, Jesus stood and said in a loud voice, "If a man is thirsty, let him come to me and drink. Whoever believes in me, as the Scripture has said, streams of living water will flow from within him." By this he meant the Spirit, whom those who believed in him were later to receive. Up to that time the Spirit had not been given, since Jesus had not yet been glorified.—Jn 7:37-39

The feeling

But whoever drinks the water I give him will never thirst. Indeed, the water I give him will become in him a spring of water welling up to eternal life.—Jn 4:14

On the day of Pentecost this gift of the Holy Ghost was given to the church. It was "poured out" upon the church, as the sunlight is shed forth upon the world.

Then Peter stood up with the Eleven, raised his voice and addressed the crowd: "Fellow Jews and all of you who are in Jerusalem, let me explain this to you; listen carefully to what I say. These men are not drunk, as you suppose. It's only nine in the morning! No, this is what was spoken by the prophet Joel: / 'In the last days, God says, / I will pour out my Spirit on all people. / Your sons and daughters will prophesy, / your young men will see visions, / your old men will dream dreams. / Even on my servants, both men and women, / I will pour out my Spirit in those days, / and they will prophesy.'"—Acts 2:14-18

Not only a few disciples, but "on all people" was the Spirit shed forth, and all who will receive the gift, may have it.

When the people heard this, they were cut to the heart and said to Peter and the other apostles, "Brothers, what shall we do?"
Peter replied, "Repent and be baptized, every one of you, in the

name of Jesus Christ so that your sins may be forgiven. And you will receive the gift of the Holy Spirit. The promise is for you and your children and for all who are far off—for all whom the Lord our God will call.—Acts 2:37-39

The Holy Spirit, like the sunlight, is free to all. The world is full of sunlight, but the plant in a cellar dwindles and dies for lack of it. What is needed is not a new outpouring of the sunlight, but the placing of the plant in the sunlight which is already poured out. It is not that God must give anything more, but that we must receive more of that which he has already given.

Do not get drunk on wine, which leads to debauchery. Instead, be filled with the Spirit.—Eph 5:18

"Be filled" yourselves, with that Spirit which fills all the earth around you. Do not ask for more of the Spirit, but let the Spirit have more of you.

This is the fact; that the Holy Spirit *is* given. Faith believes this, and by believing receives; and after faith comes the conscious sealing.

And you also were included in Christ when you heard the word of truth, the gospel of your salvation. Having believed, you were marked in him with a seal, the promised Holy Spirit.
—Eph 1:13 (Gal 3:2)

5. The presence of God.

The fact

...teaching them to obey everything I have commanded you. And surely I will be with you always, to the very end of the age.
—Mt 28:20

Where can I go from your Spirit? / Where can I flee from your presence? / If I go up to the heavens, you are there; / if I make my bed in the depths, you are there. / If I rise on the wings of the dawn, / if I settle on the far side of the sea, / even there your hand will guide me, / your right hand will hold me fast. / If I say,

"Surely the darkness will hide me / and the light become night around me," / even the darkness is as light to you. / For you created my inmost being; / you knit me together in my mother's womb.—Ps 139:7-13

The faith

The Lord Almighty is with us; / the God of Jacob is our fortress.—Ps 46:7

I will say of the Lord, "He is my refuge and my fortress, / my God, in whom I trust."—Ps 91:2 (Ps 46:1)

The feeling

Therefore we will not fear, though the earth give way / and the mountains fall into the heart of the sea.—Ps 46:2

God has said, / "Never will I leave you; / never will I forsake you." / So we say with confidence, / "The Lord is my helper; I will not be afraid. / What can man do to me?"—Heb 13:5-6

What he "has said," we may indeed "say with confidence," therefore our faith must assert unswervingly that fact of God's abiding presence with us. And as a result of this faith we shall sooner or later realize a conscious feeling of his presence. He is not present because we *feel* it, but we feel it because we believe the fact of his presence.

This divine order of the three F's, i.e., first fact, second faith, third feeling, applies to every aspect and every stage of our experience in heavenly things.

No amount of feeling is good for anything unless it is the result of faith in a divine fact; which fact is true anyhow, whether we believe it or not.

Let us get our facts then. And let us once and for all give up every idea that our feelings are the test and measure of these facts.

The facts, when believed in, will control our feelings; but no amount of feeling, no matter how fervent, can control the facts, so much as a feather's weight.

A Christian who had had a very joyous experience in a meeting, came to the minister the next day looking very downcast and said, "In your meeting yesterday I was filled with joy, and I thought I should never be sad again; but now it is all gone and I am in the depths. What is the matter with me? Has God forsaken me?" "Did you ever pass through a tunnel?" asked the minister. "Certainly I have," replied the man, "but I do not see what that has to do with it." "When you were in the tunnel did you think the sun had been blotted out and existed no longer?" continued the minister. "No, of course I did not," said the man. "I knew the sun was in the sky just the same, although I could not see it just then. But what has that to do with my experience?" "Were you very much depressed while you were going through the dark tunnel?" "No I was not, I knew I should get out into the light again soon." "And did you get out?" asked the minister. "I am out now!" exclaimed the man joyfully. "I see what you mean. The facts are just the same, no matter how I feel, and I am to rejoice in the facts not in my feelings, I see! I see!"

Let us reject then the clamorings of our feelings which declare that God's facts are but dreams of the imagination, and let us take our stand without wavering on the unalterable verities of "God's testimony," receiving it with at least as much confidence as we accord to the witness of men, and resting our souls absolutely on what he has said.

In hope, against all human hope,
    Self desperate, I believe;
Thy quickening word shall raise me up,
    Thou wilt thy Spirit give.

The thing surpasses all my thought,
    But faithful is my Lord;
Through unbelief I stagger not,
    For God hath spoke the word.

Faith, mighty faith, the promise sees,
   And looks at that alone;
Laughs at impossibilities,
   And cries—"It shall be done!"

NINE

Our Relationships
with God

Foundation Text— *Not that I have already obtained all this, or have already been made perfect, but I press on to take hold of that for which Christ Jesus took hold of me.* —Phil 3:12

Someone has said that the only thing necessary for the children of God to do in order to enter into full possession of their inheritance, is simply to *be* what they *are*. That is, in other words, to "take hold of that for which Christ Jesus took hold of me." In all human relations this principle holds good. If a man is a king in fact, he must *be* one in actual outward recognition, or his kingship avails him nothing. If a man really possesses wealth, he must act and live as a wealthy man, or his riches are of no worth to him. In all conditions of life, our success depends upon this little point of *being* what we really are.

> For you were once darkness, but now you are light in the Lord. Live as children of light. —Eph 5:8

You *are* children of light, now walk as such. That is; *be* what you *are*.

In our relations with God this is especially necessary, because these all exist in the unseen spiritual region, and can of course only be real to us as our faith makes them so. It is essential then to our peace, and also to our well-being, that we should intelligently take hold of and live out that for which Christ Jesus took hold of us. That is, we must find out what are our relationships to God, and then we must *be* just what they are. For instance, if God says I am his child, then I must *be* a child; if he says I am a king, then I must *be* kingly; and so on in all the relations which exist in the soul life.

It is of vital importance therefore that we should find out what we really *are,* in order that we may know what we ought to *be.* And this we can do by looking at the names by which he calls us.

> The man who enters by the gate is the shepherd of his sheep. The watchman opens the gate for him, and the sheep listen to his voice. He calls his own sheep by name and leads them out.—Jn 10:2-3

He "calls his own sheep by name." God's naming always means character or position. He has no fancy nor arbitrary names. Just as we never call a man a farmer unless he is a farmer, so likewise when God calls us by a name, it is because we *are* that which he calls us. The names he has given us, therefore, will tell us what we are.

> No longer will you be called Abram; your name will be Abraham, for I have made you a father of many nations.—Gn 17:5

(Abram means "father of height," and Abraham means "father of multitudes.")

> May my lord pay no attention to that wicked man Nabal. He is just like his name—his name is Fool, and folly goes with him. But as for me, your servant, I did not see the men my master sent.
> —1 Sm 25:25

(Nabal means, a "fool.")

> Then the man said, "Your name will no longer be Jacob, but

Israel, because you have struggled with God and with men and have overcome."—Gn 32:28

(Jacob means a "supplanter," and Israel means, "a prince with God.")

But now, this is what the Lord says— / he who created you, O Jacob, / he who formed you, O Israel: / "Fear not, for I have redeemed you; / I have called you by name; you are mine."
—Is 43:1

Let us see then what are some of the names by which God has called us, that we may learn to know what we really are in his sight.

1. He calls us his *children.*
2. He calls us his *heirs.*
3. He calls us his *friends.*
4. He calls us his *brethren.*
5. He calls us his *sheep.*
6. He likens us to *birds.*
7. He likens us to *chickens.*
8. He calls us *branches of the vine.*
9. He likens us to *trees.*
10. He likens us to *flowers.*
11. He calls us *clay.*
12. He calls us *vessels.*
13. He calls us *instruments.*
14. He calls us his *treasure.*
15. He calls us his *bride.*
16. Finally, he declares that we are *one* with himself.

In every one of these names there is included a whole world of comfort to those who consent to *be* what they are thus *called.*

We will look at them a little in detail, and see what is really included in this naming.

1. He calls us his *children.*

You are all sons of God through faith in Christ Jesus.—Gal 3:26

The Spirit himself testifies with our spirit that we are God's children.—Rom 8:16

Let us *be* children then in the blessed ease, and security, and childlikeness of childhood. Let us take the children's happy place of freedom from care, and from anxiety; and let us live as the children do, in the present moment, without taking thought for tomorrow.

2. He calls us his *heirs.*

Now if we are children, then we are heirs—heirs of God and co-heirs with Christ, if indeed we share in his sufferings in order that we may also share in his glory.—Rom 8:17

So you are no longer a slave, but a son; and since you are a son, God has made you also an heir.—Gal 4:7

Let us *be* heirs then in the sense of entering into possession of our inheritance. No earthly heir fails or delays to take possession of that which he inherits. He may be amazed at the good fortune which has befallen him, he may feel himself to be utterly unworthy of it; but nevertheless, if he is the heir, he takes possession of his inheritance, and rejoices in it. And we who are declared to be the heirs of God, must do the same.

3. He calls us his *friends.*

I no longer call you servants, because a servant does not know his master's business. Instead, I have called you friends, for everything that I learned from my Father I have made known to you.—Jn 15:15

And the scripture was fulfilled that says, "Abraham believed God, and it was credited to him as righteousness," and he was called God's friend.—Jas 2:23

Let us *be* his friends then in the best that we know of friendship. Let us trust him, as we like our friends to trust us; let us lean on him, as we beseech our friends to lean on us; let us try to please him for love's sake, as love leads us to try to please our earthly friends. Moreover, let us recognize the blessed fact, that if we are his friends, he is necessarily our friend also, and that the sweet duties and responsibilities of friendship are upon his shoulders, as well as upon ours.

> A man of many companions may come to ruin, / but there is a friend who sticks closer than a brother.—Prv 18:24

> The Lord would speak to Moses face to face, as a man speaks with his friend.—Ex 33:11

If God is our friend, and if we are his friends, he will tell us his secrets; "I have called you friends, for everything that I learned from my Father I have made known to you" (Jn 15:15). (Compare Gn 18:17, and Amos 3:7; See also, Ps 25:14.) If we would learn the Lord's secrets, therefore, we must be his friends; and he himself has told us how. "You are my friends if you do whatsoever I command you."

4. He calls us his *brothers*.

> Both the one who makes men holy and those who are made holy are of the same family. So Jesus is not ashamed to call them brothers. He says, / "I will declare your name to my brothers; / in the presence of the congregation I will sing your praises.
> —Heb 2:11-12

Let us *be* his brothers, then, and take to our hearts the wonderful comfort and joy of having such an "elder Brother" to bear our burdens and share our sorrows. Some of us know the comfort of an earthly brother; let us realize the comfort of the heavenly brother as well.

> For those God foreknew he also predestined to be conformed to the likeness of his Son, that he might be the firstborn among many brothers.—Rom 8:29

Since he is the firstborn in the family, we, who are the younger members of it, have surely a right to look to him for all that belongs to an elder brother's place, and may without hesitation make use of him as our brother; and lay upon him a brother's burdens.

5. He calls us his *sheep*.

You my sheep, the sheep of my pasture, are people, and I am your God, declares the Sovereign Lord.—Ez 34:31 (Ps 95:7)

Let us *be* sheep then, and abandon ourselves to the care of the Shepherd to whom we belong. The sheep cannot care for themselves, nor protect themselves, nor provide food for themselves; the Shepherd must do it all. The responsibility of their well-being is all on his shoulders, not on theirs. They have nothing to do but to trust him, and to follow him. And the Lord is *our* Shepherd.

A great many people refuse to be the sheep, and insist upon trying to be the Shepherd instead. That is, they try to assume all the duties that belong to the Shepherd; and they entirely decline to be cared for and protected as the sheep are. Or else they try to be both the sheep and also the Shepherd, and to perform the part of each at the same time, an impossible and wearisome task. Let us cease then trying to be anything but just simply what we are; sheep in the care of the Divine Shepherd.

6. He likens us to *birds*.

Look at the birds of the air; they do not sow or reap or store away in barns, and yet your heavenly Father feeds them. Are you not much more valuable than they?—Mt 6:26

Are not five sparrows sold for two pennies? Yet not one of them is forgotten by God. Indeed, the very hairs of your head are all numbered. Don't be afraid; you are worth more than many sparrows.—Lk 12:6-7

We are to "look at the birds of the air" that we may learn to live a life of freedom and of joy such as theirs, in the glad consciousness of our heavenly Father's watchful care and protecting love. Let us say then with the poet,

It cometh, therefore, to this, Lord,
That I *have* considered thy word,
And I will henceforth be thy bird.

7. He likens us to *chicks*.

"O Jerusalem, Jerusalem, you who kill the prophets and stone those sent to you, how often I have longed to gather your children together, as a hen gathers her chicks under her wings, but you were not willing." —Mt 23:37

The little chicken hides itself under the fortress of its mother's wings, and feels safe, no matter what enemies may be raging around; and we also may hide "under his wings," and have no fear. Suppose a little chicken should stand off trembling and frightened, when the hawk was in sight, refusing to go under the mother's wing, because it was too small and insignificant and helpless. Would not the mother's call say to it as plainly as words could speak, "It is just because you *are* little and helpless, that I want you under my wing. If you were strong and capable of protecting yourself, you would not need my wing." And does not God say the same in effect to us? Our helplessness and littleness constitute our right to his care. Let us then consent to *be* the little chickens, hidden under the blessed fortress of his divine wing.

He will cover you with his feathers, / and under his wings you will find refuge; / his faithfulness will be your shield and rampart.
—Ps 91:4

8. He calls us *branches* of the vine.

I am the true vine and my Father is the gardener. He cuts off every branch in me that bears no fruit, while every branch that does bear fruit he trims clean so that it will be even more fruitful. You are already clean because of the word I have spoken to you. Remain in me, and I will remain in you. No branch can bear fruit by itself; it must remain in the vine. Neither can you bear fruit unless you remain in me. I am the vine; you are the branches. If a man remains in me and I in him, he will bear much fruit; apart from me you can do nothing.—Jn 15:1-5

Be branches then, and realize that you have no life apart from the vine: and realize also that you have nothing to do in order to bring forth much fruit, but to abide in the vine. The branch cannot bear fruit of itself, in the very nature of things. Do not try, then, to do it, but abide in the vine, and let the life-giving sap flow through you, without effort on your part, and without anxiety. Only see to it that you do not hinder its flow by doubt or by rebellion. *Be* a branch and a branch only, and do not try to be anything else. Do not try to *make* the fruit, but consent to *bear* it. Let it grow.

9. He likens us to *trees*.

But blessed is the man who trusts in the Lord, / whose confidence is in him. / He will be like a tree planted by the water / that sends out its roots by the stream. / It does not fear when heat comes; / its leaves are always green. / It has no worries in a year of drought / and never fails to bear fruit.—Jer 17:7-8 (Ps 92:12-13; 1:3)

10. He likens us to *flowers*.

And why do you worry about clothes? See how the lilies of the field grow. They do not labor or spin. Yet I tell you not even Solomon in all his splendor was dressed like one of these. If that is how God clothes the grass of the field, which is here today and tomorrow is thrown into the fire, will he not much more clothe you, O you of little faith?—Mt 6:28-30 (Is 5:7)

Let us *be* trees and flowers then, and grow as they grow, in a happy unconsciousness of our growing. Let us consider them "how they grow," and let us give up all our straining, and stretching, and self-efforts after growth, and try to grow like them by the power of an inward growing-life alone.

Let us be like them also in this, that we do not try to cultivate ourselves. Too many try to be their own husbandmen, and to cultivate, and water, and dig about, and prune, and even sometimes to plant themselves. They try to *be* what they are not, and what they never can be, i.e., the husbandman instead of the branches, the gardener instead of the garden, the farmer instead of the trees and flowers. And of course they fail. But let us *be* what we are, the trees, and flowers, and gardens only, and let us leave to our Divine Husbandman all the care and responsibility of our growing and our blooming.

11. He likens us to *clay*.

Yet, O Lord, you are our Father. / We are the clay, you are the potter; / we are all the work of your hand.—Is 64:8 (Jer 18:6)

Let us *be* the clay then, and not the potter. Most people try to be both the clay and the potter. But this is an impossibility, and only mars the work. The clay must be put into the potter's hands, and abandoned to his working. The potter takes the clay thus abandoned to him, and begins to mold and fashion it to his will. The clay can do nothing but yield itself to the potter and submit to his processes: the potter alone can do the fashioning and moulding; and the responsibility for this is all on his shoulders, not on the clay. Let us consent then to *be* what we *are,* and give up forever trying to be what we are not and never can be.

Does the clay say to the potter, / "What are you making?" / Does your work say, / "He has no hands?"—Is 45:9

12. He calls us *vessels*.

If a man cleanses himself from the latter [ignoble purposes], he will be an instrument for noble purposes, made holy, useful to the Master and prepared to do any good work.
—2 Tm 2:21 (Acts 9:15)

The things that are necessary in a vessel are that it should be empty and clean. It is of comparatively little account for purposes of use, as to what is its shape or the material of which it is made. The Master can fill and use any vessel that is emptied of self and is open to receive his Spirit.

13. He calls us *instruments*.

> Do not offer the parts of your body to sin, as instruments of wickedness, but rather offer yourselves to God, as those who have been brought from death to life; and offer the parts of your body to him as instruments of righteousness.—Rom 6:13

> You are my war club, / my weapon for battle— / with you I shatter nations, / with you I destroy kingdoms.—Jer 51:20

God does not tell us that we are the workmen, who are to use and manage the instruments, but that we are the instruments to be used and managed by the Divine Master Workman who made us, and who alone, therefore, understands for what work we are best fitted, and how to use us. The only thing the instrument can do is to "yield" itself perfectly to the will of the Master Workman. Romans 6:16. The Master surely knows how best to use his instruments, and it is plainly not the business of the tool to decide these questions for itself. Neither must it try to help by its own efforts to do the work. One absolutely necessary characteristic of a tool is its pliableness. The moment resistance is felt in any tool, the moment it refuses to move just as the master wants, that moment it becomes unfit for use. If I am writing, and my fine gold pen begins to leak and to move with difficulty, I will soon lay it aside and take gladly in its place even a stub end of a lead pencil, if only it will move easily in obedience to my will. The strength of an instruments lies in its helplessness. Because it is helpless to do anything of itself, therefore the master can use it as he pleases. There must be no interference on the part of the instrument. So Paul says—

> But he said to me, "My grace is sufficient for you, for my power is made perfect in weakness." Therefore I will boast all the more gladly about my weaknesses, so that Christ's power may rest on me.—2 Cor 12:9-10

The "power of Christ" can rest fully only upon those instruments who have no power of their own.

14. He calls us his *treasure*.

For the Lord has chosen Jacob to be his own, / Israel to be his treasured possession.—Ps 135:4

Now if you obey me fully and keep my covenant, then out of all nations you will be my treasured possession. Although the whole earth is mine. . . .—Ex 19:5

If God can call us his "treasured possession" let us take the joy of it to our souls. For, dear and precious to our hearts as are those we particularly love, far more dear and precious must we ourselves be to our Father in heaven, since he calls us his "treasured possession." *We* always take special care of our treasures, and God will surely take special care of his.

15. He calls us his *bride*.

As a young man marries a maiden, / so will your sons marry you; / as a bridegroom rejoices over his bride, / so will your God rejoice over you.—Is 62:5

I will betroth you to me forever; / I will betroth you in righteousness and justice, / in love and compassion. / I will betroth you in faithfulness, / and you will acknowledge the Lord.—Hos 2:19-20 (Eph 5:23-32)

But little need be said concerning this. It gives us a sight of the love of espousals between Christ's heart and ours. Love takes different forms in our lives, and regards its object in many different ways. The love here set forth to us in this wondrous naming, is the highest and closest and most tender that human hearts can know, and it pictures to us a glory of affection between Christ's heart and ours, such as no words can adequately express. It is one of the latest revelations that come to a soul. At first we seek his *gifts* only, but at last we seek *himself*. At first we are occupied with our needs and come to the Lord simply to have them supplied. But at last we lose sight of the gifts in our longing for the Giver, and can be satisfied with nothing short of himself. Our souls cry out for a realized union with our Lord. And then there comes to us with untold joy the wonderful words, "As a Bridegroom rejoices over his bride, so will thy God rejoice over thee," and we believe them, and enter into our rest in the bosom of our Beloved!

16. Finally he declares that we are *one with himself.*

That all of them may be one, Father, just as you are in me and I am in you. May they also be in us so that the world may believe that you have sent me. I have given them the glory that you gave me, that they may be one as we are one: I in them and you in me. May they be brought to complete unity to let the world know that you sent me and have loved them even as you have loved me.
—Jn 17:21-23

"That they may be one!" it is all shut up in this! One with the Father *as* the Son is one! Similarity of thought, of feeling, of desire, of love, of hate! We may have it all, if we will. We may walk through this life so united to Christ, that our cares and our interests, our sorrows and our joys, our purposes and our wishes will be the same. One will alone to govern, and that his will. One mind alone to lead us, and that his mind. He in us, and we in him, will then be our living; until at last, so intermingled will our lives become, that we shall be able to say in truth, always and everywhere, "Not I, but Christ." For self will vanish in such a union as this, and that great "I" of ours which so fills up our present horizon, will wilt down into nothing before the glory of his overcoming presence! *Be* one, then, since he says we are, and let the power of that oneness be lived out in every moment of our existence.

Dear reader, which one of these figures expresses your relationship with the Lord? Which name have you had an ear to hear whispered in the secret of your soul?

He who has an ear, let him hear what the Spirit says to the churches. To him who overcomes, I will give some of the hidden manna. I will also give him a white stone with a new name written on it, known only to him who receives it.—Rv 2:17

Him who overcomes I will make a pillar in the temple of my God. Never again will he leave it. I will write on him the name of my God and the name of the city of my God, the new Jerusalem, which is coming down out of heaven from my God; and I will also write on him my new name.—Rv 3:12

Will we consent to let God write upon us his "new name?" And what shall it be? He awaits our answer. For he may call us what he will, but until we consent to *be* what he calls us, the new name is not *written* upon us.

Choose your relationship then, either one, or all, and henceforth *be* what you have discovered you really *are* in the mind and will of God.

TEN

Fruitfulness

Foundation Text— *You did not choose me, but I chose you to go and bear fruit—fruit that will last. Then the Father will give you whatever you ask in my name.* —Jn 15:16

God's purpose in our salvation is that we should bring forth fruit. A husbandman plants the vine for the sake of the grapes it will bear; the farmer plants his apple orchard in order to gather fruit. A fruitless Christian life is an impossibility.

I am the true vine and my Father is the gardener. He cuts off every branch in me that bears no fruit, while every branch that does bear fruit he trims clean so that it will be even more fruitful.—Jn 15:1-2

The ax is already at the root of the trees, and every tree that does not produce good fruit will be cut down and thrown into the fire.—Lk 3:9

Many are apt to think far more of being *saved,* than of being *fruitful.* But God does not separate these things; to be saved *is* to be fruitful, and to be fruitful is to be saved.

Then he told this parable: "A man had a fig tree, planted in his vineyard, and he went to look for fruit on it, but did not find any. So he said to the man who took care of the vineyard, 'For three years now I've been coming to look for fruit on this fig tree and haven't found any. Cut it down! Why should it use up the soil?'

" 'Sir,' the man replied, 'leave it alone for one more year, and I'll dig around it and fertilize it. If it bears fruit next year, fine! If not, then cut it down.' "—Lk 13:6-9 (Heb 6:7-8)

No matter how good an outward appearance our lives may make, no matter how clear our doctrines, nor how great our activities, unless we "bear fruit" we cannot be acceptable to God. And the fruit he desires is character. It is to *be* right even more than to *do* right. Of course the doing will follow the being, but the vital point is the being. Most people have too much reversed this order, and have made the *doing* the vital thing; limiting the meaning of fruit-bearing to service, so much work done, so many meetings held, so many sermons preached or prayers prayed, such and such results accomplished. But God's primary idea of fruit is Christ-likeness.

But the fruit of the Spirit is love, joy, peace, patience, kindness, goodness, faithfulness, gentleness and self-control. Against such things there is no law.—Gal 5:22-23

And this is my prayer: that your love may abound more and more in knowledge and depth of insight, so that you may be able to discern what is best and may be pure and blameless until the day of Christ, filled with the fruit of righteousness that comes through Jesus Christ—to the glory and praise of God.
—Phil 1:9-11 (Rom 8:29; Eph 5:9)

People may do much wonderful so-called Christian work, and yet in it all bear not one single "fruit of righteousness" that will be "to the glory and praise of God."

But the wisdom that comes from heaven is first of all pure; then peace loving, considerate, submissive, full of mercy and good fruit, impartial and sincere. Peacemakers who sow in peace raise a harvest of righteousness.—Jas 3:17-18 (Mt 7:16-20)

Some Christians have what is sometimes called a "public gift," and can speak or pray in a meeting to great edification; but they go home to be cross to their families, and bitter towards their acquaintances, and fault-finding, and malicious, and full of self. They have great outward results apparently, but they have not as yet the very first and most vital of all the "fruits of the Spirit," which is love; and consequently all the rest, grand as they may seem, profit them nothing.

If I speak in the tongues of men and of angels, but have not love, I am only a resounding gong or a clanging cymbal. If I have the gift of prophecy and can fathom all mysteries and all knowledge, and if I have a faith that can move mountains, but have not love, I am nothing. If I give all I possess to the poor and surrender my body to the flames, but have not love, I gain nothing.
—1 Cor 13:1-3

Israel was a spreading vine; / he brought forth fruit for himself. / As his fruit increased, / he built more altars; / as his land prospered, / he adorned his sacred stones.—Hos 10:1

To bring "forth fruit for himself" means simply that self is the center and end of all the work. To bring glory to self, to gain advantage for self, to secure future rewards for self, to exalt self in some way, this is the secret end and aim of such service.

Make a tree good and its fruit will be good, or make a tree bad and its fruit will be bad, for a tree is recognized by its fruit. You brood of vipers, how can you who are evil say anything good? For out of the overflow of the heart the mouth speaks. The good man brings good things out of the good stored up in him, and the evil man brings evil things out of the evil stored up in him.
—Mt 12:33-35

In the very nature of things it is impossible for an "evil man" to bring forth good things; for, even though we do not know it and surely do not intend it, yet it is nevertheless an inexorable fact that "out of the overflow of the heart" the life will be lived. We cannot "put on" in spiritual things. If our tree is corrupt, our fruit will be corrupt also, no matter how much we may try to train it up or make it appear well.

No good tree bears bad fruit, nor does a bad tree bear good fruit. Each tree is recognized by its own fruit. People do not pick figs from thornbushes, or grapes from briers. The good man brings good things out of the good stored up in his heart, and the evil man brings evil things out of the evil stored up in his heart. For out of the overflow of his heart his mouth speaks.
—Lk 6:43-46

If the fruits of the Spirit, which are love, and gentleness, and meekness, and long-suffering, are not seen in a man's life, then the Spirit cannot be there either, for where the Spirit is, his fruits must necessarily be manifest.

But when he saw many of the Pharisees and Sadducees coming to where he was baptizing, he said to them: "You brood of vipers! Who warned you to flee from the coming wrath? Produce fruit in keeping with repentance. And do not think you can say to yourselves, 'We have Abraham as our father.' I tell you that out of these stones God can raise up children for Abraham. The ax is already at the root of the trees, and every tree that does not produce good fruit will be cut down and thrown into the fire.
—Mt 3:7-10

Even to have "Abraham as our father" will not save us, neither will any other outward relation or position. Nothing but the fruits of the Spirit can come from the Spirit; and without these fruits, no one can claim to be walking in the Spirit, let their outward activities or eminence in the church be what they may.

Since they hated knowledge / and did not choose to fear the Lord, / since they would not accept my advice / and spurned my rebuke, / they will eat the fruit of their ways / and be filled with the fruit of their schemes.—Prv 1:29-31

The "fruit of their ways" may look like goodly fruit to the eye of flesh, but the soul that is compelled to "eat" of it, will find itself starved as to its true inner life.

I the Lord search the mind / and try the heart, / to give to every man according to his ways, / according to the fruit of his doings.—Jer 17:10 (RSV)

Man may judge by outward appearances, but the Lord "searches the heart," and gives to each one of us according to the fruit he finds *there.*

We who are Christian workers need especially to realize this. We need to understand that no amount of preaching or praying, or singing, or weeping, or groaning will do, instead of being gentle, and meek, and long suffering, and good. A great many people want to work for the Lord, but do not want to be good for him; but it is the goodness he cares for, far more than the work. If you cannot do both, choose the being good, for it is infinitely more important.

I will sing for the one I love / a song about his vineyard: / My loved one had a vineyard / on a fertile hillside. / He dug it up and cleared it of stones / and planted it with the choicest vines. / He built a watchtower in it / and cut out a winepress as well. / Then he looked for a crop of good grapes, / but it yielded only bad fruit. / "Now you dwellers in Jerusalem and men of Judah, / judge between me and my vineyard. / What more could have been done for my vineyard / than I have done for it? / When I looked for good grapes, / why did it yield only bad? / Now I will tell you / what I am going to do to my vineyard: / I will take away its hedge, / and it will be destroyed; / I will break down its wall, / and it will be trampled. / I will make it a wasteland, / neither pruned nor cultivated, / and briers and thorns will grow there. / I will command the clouds / not to rain on it." / The vineyard of the Lord Almighty / is the house of Israel, / and the men of Judah / are the garden of his delight. / And he looked for justice, but saw bloodshed; / for righteousness, but heard cries of distress.

—Is 5:1-7

We must see to it that the fruit we bring forth in our lives does not partake of the nature of "wild grapes," which set the teeth of all with whom we live in our everyday lives, on edge. There *are* alas! too many such Christians to be found, even sometimes among those who are pillars in the Church.

> Their vine comes from the vine of Sodom / and from the fields of Gomorrah. / Their grapes are filled with poison, / and their clusters with bitterness.—Dt 32:32 (Jer 2:21)

How then does this "good fruit" come? There is only one way in which it *can* come. It grows from the seed God plants.

> He also said, "This is what the kingdom of God is like. A man scatters seed on the ground. Night and day, whether he sleeps or gets up, the seed sprouts and grows, though he does not know how. All by itself the soil produces grain—first the stalk, then the head, then the full kernel in the head. As soon as the grain is ripe, he puts the sickle to it, because the harvest has come."
> Again he said, "What shall we say the kingdom of God is like, or what parable shall we use to describe it? It is like a mustard seed, which is the smallest seed you plant in the ground. Yet when planted, it grows and becomes the largest of all garden plants, with such big branches that the birds of the air can perch in its shade."—Mk 4:26-32 (Mk 4:2-8)

Fruit does not come by effort, but by growth. It unfolds from within. There must be first a good inward life, before there can be good outward fruit. What would we think of a farmer who should make an orchard by beginning at the apples; and should collect bushel after bushel of excellent fruit, should tie these on branches, and fasten the branches to tree trunks, and then fasten the trunks to the roots, and finally plant the trees thus made, in the ground? And yet this would not be more foolish than it is to try to begin the Christian life at the works end instead of the character end.

> Who of you by worrying can add a single hour to his life?
> And why do you worry about clothes? See how the lilies of the field grow. They do not labor or spin. Yet I tell you that not even Solomon in all his splendor was dressed like one of these. If that is how God clothes the grass of the field, which is here today and tomorrow is thrown into the fire, will he not much more clothe you, O you of little faith:—Mt 6:27-30

> A good tree cannot bear bad fruit, and a bad tree cannot bear good fruit.—Mt 7:18

Notice the word "cannot" in this passage. It does not say will not, but cannot. It expresses an impossibility, in the very nature of things. No outward "putting on" therefore will avail anything in the matter of fruit bearing. The tree itself must be good, or the fruit it bears "cannot" be good, try as hard as we may.

Some people always walk on spiritual stilts when before others. If they are riding in a railway car, they take out their Bibles in order to look pious; when they write a letter, they try to put in some expressions that will show their religion; they interlard their conversation with pious ejaculations. They can never afford to be natural in the presence of others, for fear they should not be considered as religious as they really are. They do their works to be "seen by men," and they do indeed have their reward. Man sees and praises; but God sees and condemns.

> Be careful not to do your "acts of righteousness" before men, to be seen by them. If you do, you will have no reward from your Father in heaven.
> So when you give to the needy, do not announce it with trumpets, as the hypocrites do in the synagogues and on the streets, to be honored by men. I tell you the truth, they have received their reward in full. But when you give to the needy, do not let your left hand know what your right hand is doing, so that your giving may be in secret. Then your Father who sees what is done in secret, will reward you.
> But when you pray, do not be like the hypocrites, for they love to pray standing in the synagogues and on the street corners to be seen by men. I tell you the truth, they have received their reward in full. —Mt 6:1-5

A man can never be more than his character makes him. A man can never do more nor better than deliver or embody that which is his character. Nothing valuable can come out of a man that is not first in the man. Character must stand behind and back up every thing, the sermon, the poem, the picture, the book. None of them is worth a straw without it.

Out of the same mouth come praise and cursing. My brothers, this should not be. Can both fresh water and salt water flow from the same spring? My brothers, can a fig tree bear olives, or a grapevine bear figs? Neither can a salt spring produce fresh water.

Who is wise and understanding among you? Let him show it by his good life, by deeds done in the humility that comes from wisdom. But if you harbor bitter envy and selfish ambition in your hearts, do not boast about it or deny the truth. Such "wisdom" does not come down from heaven but is earthly, unspiritual, of the devil. For where you have envy and selfish ambition, there you find disorder and every evil practice.

But the wisdom that comes from heaven is first of all pure; then peace loving, considerate, submissive, full of mercy and good fruit, impartial and sincere. Peacemakers who sow in peace raise a harvest of righteousness. —Jas 3:10-18 (Mt 15:16-20)

Character then is the essential thing. What is in the heart, and what comes out of the heart are the only realities in life. And if we fail to see this, we are yet, as our Lord has said, without understanding. In the very nature of things a fig tree cannot bear both figs and thistles, and neither likewise can blessing and cursing be the fruit of the same spirit.

No one can serve two masters. Either he will hate the one and love the other, or he will be devoted to the one and despise the other. You cannot serve both God and Money.
—Mt 6:24 (Rom 6:20-22)

What then is the secret of true fruit-bearing?

Remain in me, and I will remain in you. No branch can bear fruit by itself; it must remain in the vine. Neither can you bear fruit unless you remain in me.

I am the vine; you are the branches. If a man remains in me and I in him, he will bear much fruit; apart from me you can do nothing. If anyone does not remain in me, he is like a branch that is thrown away and withers; such branches are picked up, thrown into the fire and burned. If you remain in me and my words remain in you, ask whatever you wish, and it will be given you. This is to my Father's glory, that you bear much fruit, showing yourselves to be my disciples. —Jn 15:4-8

Here again we have the inexorable nature of things, "No branch can bear fruit by itself." Try as hard as we may, no fruit is possible unless we remain in Christ. Other things *are* possible; wonderful works perhaps, eminent service, great benevolences, but not the "fruit of the Spirit." This fruit cannot come from any other source than from the indwelling Spirit.

"I will be like the dew to Israel; / he will blossom like a lily. / Like a cedar of Lebanon / he will send down his roots; / his young shoots will grow. / His splendor will be like an olive tree, / his fragrance like a cedar of lebanon. / Men will dwell again in his shade. / He will flourish like the grain. / He will blossom like a vine, / and his fame will be like the wine from Lebanon. / O Ephraim, what more have I to do with idols? / I will answer him and care for him. / I am like a green pine tree; / your fruitfulness comes from me." / Who is wise? He will realize these things. / Who is discerning? He will understand them. / The ways of the Lord are right; / the righteous walk in them, / but the rebellious stumble in them.—Hos 14:5-8 (Rom 7:4-5; Is 27:6)

"Your fruitfulness comes from me," not from anything of the flesh, not from our own activities, not from anything of self in any way, but from God alone. And he alone can perfect his own fruit.

He cuts off every branch in me that bears no fruit, while every branch that does bear fruit he trims clean so that it will be even more fruitful.—Jn 15:2

It is the husbandman's business to prune and purge the vine in order to make it fruitful. And we must accept all the storms and sorrows of life as the purgings necessary to make us bring forth more fruit. To an inexperienced eye the trimming and cutting of the gardener often seem ruthless, and we cry out to him to spare the vine. But in the autumn, when the rich clusters of fruit are hanging from the same vine, we acknowledge his wisdom and applaud his skill. And in our soul life we may similarly be tempted sometimes to question the wisdom or the goodness of the Divine Husbandman, when he sees it necessary to cut off our most flourishing branches, or to trim our life of its dearest joys. But the Husbandman knows what is best for his vine and we must leave it all to him.

For our light and momentary troubles are achieving for us an eternal glory that far outweighs them all. —2 Cor 4:17

And you have forgotten that word of encouragement that addresses you as sons: "My son, do not make light of the Lord's discipline, / and do not lose heart when he rebukes you, / because the Lord disciplines those he loves, / and he punishes everyone he accepts as a son." / Endure hardship as discipline; God is treating you as sons. For what son is not disciplined by his father? If you are not disciplined (and everyone undergoes discipline), then you are illegitimate children and not true sons. Moreover, we have all had human fathers who disciplined us and we respected them for it. How much more should we submit to the Father of our spirits and live! Our fathers disciplined us for a little while as they thought best; but God disciplines us for our good, that we may share in his holiness. No discipline seems pleasant at the time, but painful. Later on, however, it produces a harvest of righteousness and peace for those who have been trained by it. —Heb 12:5-11

What then must we do if we would bring forth "much fruit?"

1. We must abandon ourselves to the Lord and trust him perfectly.

But blessed is the man who trusts in the Lord, / whose confidence is in him. / He will be like a tree planted by the water / that sends out its roots by the stream. / It does not fear when heat comes; / its leaves are always green. / It has no worries in a year of drought / and never fails to bear fruit. —Jer 17:7-8 (Ps 1:1-4)

2. We must receive the truth and believe it; and must keep on steadfastly believing it, against all seemings.

This is the meaning of the parable: The seed is the word of God. Those along the path are the ones who hear, and then the devil comes and takes away the word from their hearts, so that they cannot believe and be saved. Those on the rock are the ones who

receive the word with joy when they hear it, but they have no root. They believe for a while, but in the time of testing they fall away. The seed that fell among thorns stands for those who hear, but as they go on their way they are choked by life's worries, riches and pleasures, and they do not mature. But the seed on good soil stands for those with a noble and good heart, who hear the word, retain it, and by persevering produce a crop.
—Lk 8:11-15 (Dt 7:12-14; Lv 26:14-15, 20)

3. We must submit ourselves to God's will, and must obey his voice.

If you follow my decrees and are careful to obey my commands, I will send you rain in its season, and the ground will yield its crops and the trees of the field their fruit. Your threshing will continue until grape harvest and the grape harvest will continue until planting, and you will eat all the food you want and live in safety in your land.—Lv 26:3-5 (Dt 28:2-5, 11)

4. We must die as to the self-life, and must be alive only to the indwelling life of Christ.

I tell you the truth, unless a kernel of wheat falls to the ground and dies, it remains only a single seed. But if it dies, it produces many seeds. The man who loves his life will lose it, while the man who hates his life in this world will keep it for eternal life.
—Jn 12:24-25

He himself bore our sins in his body on the tree, so that we might die to sins and live for righteousness; by his wounds you have been healed.—1 Pt 2:24 (Rom 7:5-6)

In order to bring forth the fruits of the Spirit, we must live in the Spirit, and must die to all that is of the flesh. If we would bear fruit to God, we must cease to bear fruit to self.

Those who belong to Christ Jesus have crucified the sinful nature with its passions and desires. Since we live by the Spirit, let us keep in step with the Spirit.—Gal 5:24-25 (Eph 4:22-24)

While however the primary sense of fruit-bearing is character, there is also a fruitfulness in service that follows as the outcome of this inward life.

Fruit always covers a seed, and a new growth will therefore invariably follow in the wake of all fruit-bearing. The fruit is simply the wrapping which is around the seed; and if your fruit-bearing is real, and not fictitious, there will be sown by your living, seeds of life in the world around you that will spring up in wondrous fruitfulness in the hearts of others.

> For this reason, since the day we heard about you, we have not stopped praying for you and asking God to fill you with the knowledge of his will through all spiritual wisdom and understanding. And we pray this in order that you may live a life worthy of the Lord and may please him in every way: bearing fruit in every good work, growing in the knowledge of God. —Col 1:9-10

> Through Jesus, therefore, let us continually offer to God a sacrifice of praise—the fruit of lips that confess his name.
> —Heb 13:15 (Ez 34:26-27; Zec 8:12-13)

Does *your* fruit cover a seed of good? Is there so much sweetness, and gentleness, and meekness, and love, in *your* daily living as to be a seed of blessing in the hearts of your family, and friends, and neighbors? Or does your life sow seeds of hatred, and anger, and all unlovely and un-Christlike things?

> Do not be deceived: God cannot be mocked. A man reaps what he sows. The one who sows to please his sinful nature, from that nature will reap destruction; the one who sows to please the Spirit, from the Spirit will reap eternal life. Let us not become weary in doing good, for at the proper time we will reap a harvest if we do not give up.—Gal 6:7-9

There is no more solemn fact in all the universe than this, that what a man sows that shall he also reap. And the only escape from it is to be found in the rooting out of the seed which has been sown to the flesh, and the planting of a new crop. We must begin to bring forth fruit unto God and from God only, that is those divine fruits of the Spirit whose seed will spring up in blessing for all around us.

In the same way, let your light shine before men, that they may see your good deeds and praise your Father in heaven.—Mt 5:16

You were bought at a price. Therefore honor God with your body.—1 Cor 6:20 (2 Cor 3:3)

It may well be that our Divine Husbandman is seeking fruit at this very moment from many of the trees of his planting, and is finding none, in spite of a great outward show of greenness and vigor.

The next day as they were leaving Bethany, Jesus was hungry. Seeing in the distance a fig tree in leaf, he went to find out if it had any fruit. When he reached it, he found nothing but leaves, because it was not the season for figs.—Mk 11:12-13

Jesus said to them, "Have you never read in the Scriptures: / " 'The stone the builders rejected / has become the capstone; / the Lord has done this, / and it is marvelous in our eyes?' / "Therefore I tell you that the kingdom of God will be taken away / from you and given to a people who will produce its fruit.
—Mt 21:41-43 (Jude 1:12)

From many an active Christian has the kingdom been taken, to their great surprise; but the secret of it, if looked for, would be found in this simple fact, that that Christian has not been producing its fruit.

But let *us* be among the number of those whose fruit shall be so truly "the fruit of the Spirit" as to be always to the praise of God's glory.

You are a garden locked up, my sister, my bride; / you are a spring enclosed, a sealed fountain. / Your plants are an orchard of pomegranates / with choice fruits, / with henna and nard, / nard and saffron, / calamus and cinnamon, / with every kind of incense tree, / with myrrh and aloes / and all the finest spices. / You are a garden fountain, / a well of flowing water / streaming down from Lebanon.—Sg 4:12-15 (Ps 92:12-14)

And let us be content with whatever purging or pruning our Divine Husbandman may see to be necessary for our perfecting, anxious only to "lay up pleasant fruits" for our beloved, that he may see of the travail of his soul in us and be satisfied.

> Awake, north wind, / and come, south wind! / Blow on my garden, / that its fragrance may spread abroad. / Let my lover come into his garden / and taste its choice fruits.—Sg 4:16

> I have come into my garden, my sister, my bride; / I have gathered my myrrh with my spice. / I have eaten my honeycomb and my honey; / I have drunk my wine and my milk.—Sg 5:1

> The mandrakes send out their fragrance, and at our door is every delicacy, / both new and old, / that I have stored up for you, my lover.—Sg 7:13

ELEVEN

We Are Servants

Foundation Text: *Again, it will be like a man going on a journey, who called his servants and entrusted his property to them.* —Mt 25:14

This is a parable concerning service, and is full of most important teaching. "His servants" must mean disciples, followers, in other words, Christians. Evidently *all* the servants were called. None were left out, none were expected to pass the time of the Master's absence in idleness. And therefore if you are in the household, the call is to you. No member of the household is excepted. None can excuse themselves because they have not been called, for the call is to every one.

> It's like a man going away: he leaves his house in charge of his servants, each with his assigned task, and tells the one at the door to keep watch.—Mk 13:34

"Each with his assigned task." Not the same task to all, but each one has his own talent and his own place. And each one is responsible only for that which is given to *him himself* to do. This seems too plain to be spoken of; but as a fact, most members of God's household are more concerned about the work given to someone else, than about that given to themselves.

When Peter saw him, he asked, "Lord, what about him?"
Jesus answered, "If I want him to remain alive until I return,
what is that to you? You must follow me."—Jn 21:21-22

Not what others do or leave undone, but what I myself do or
leave undone, is the vital thing in my soul life.

Neither should I care for the judgment of others concerning
my work. A servant in a household is not anxious to know what
the master or mistress next door may think of him or his work,
but only what his own master and mistress think.

I care very little if I am judged by you or by any human court;
indeed, I do not even judge myself. My conscience is clear, but
that does not make me innocent. It is the Lord who judges me.
Therefore judge nothing before the appointed time; wait till the
Lord comes. He will bring to light what is hidden in darkness and
will expose the motives of men's hearts. At that time each will
receive his praise from God.—1 Cor 4:3-5

Only One who can see the end from the beginning is able to
judge a righteous judgment; therefore the servants of Christ
must reserve their judgment of one another, until the final
judgment is declared by their common Master. And we are
therefore in truth forbidden to judge at all.

Who are you to judge someone else's servant? To his own master
he stands or falls. And he will stand, for the Lord is able to make
him stand.—Rom 14:4

Brothers, do not slander one another. Anyone who speaks against
his brother or judges him speaks against the law and judges it.
When you judge the law, you are not keeping it, but sitting in
judgment on it.—Jas 4:11

Do not judge, or you too will be judged. For in the same way you
judge others, you will be judged, and with the measure you use, it
will be measured to you.

Why do you look at the speck of sawdust in your brother's eye
and pay no attention to the plank in your own eye? How can you
say to your brother, "Let me take the speck out of your eye," when
all the time there is a plank in your own eye? You hypocrite, first

take the plank out of your own eye, and then you will see clearly to remove the speck from your brother's eye.—Mt 7:1-5

We are each one to do our own work faithfully, without regard to how our fellow workers may do theirs. If these plain and positive rules were followed in the church of Christ, what a millenium of peace we should have!

> You, then, why do you judge your brother? Or why do you look down on your brother? For we will all stand before God's judgment seat. It is written: / " 'As surely as I live,' says the Lord, / 'Every knee will bow before me; / every tongue will confess to God.' " / So then, each of us will give an account of himself to God. / Therefore let us stop passing judgment on one another. Instead, make up your mind not to put any stumbling block or obstacle in your brother's way.—Rom 14:10-13

Our only judging must be lest we ourselves put a stumbling-block in our brother's way. What wonderful Christian harmony such judging as this would cause!

> He said: "A man of noble birth went to a distant country to have himself appointed king and then to return. So he called ten of his servants and gave them ten minas. 'Put this money to work,' he said, 'until I come back.' "—Lk 19:12-13

Of course, the object of the Master in giving talents to his servants, is that they should "put them to work" until his return. But we must notice that the talents were not all alike.

> "To one he gave five talents of money, to another two talents, and to another one talent, each according to his ability. Then he went on his journey."—Mt 25:15

"Each according to his ability." All are not capable of the same work, and the Master's gifts are apportioned to us, according to our individual capacity.

> There are different kinds of gifts, but the same Spirit. There are different kinds of service, but the same Lord. There are different

kinds of working, but the same God works all of them in all men. Now to each one the manifestation of the Spirit is given for the common good. To one there is given through the Spirit the message of wisdom, to another the message of knowledge by means of the same Spirit, to another faith by the same Spirit, to another gifts of healing by that one Spirit, to another miraculous powers, to another prophecy, to another the ability to distinguish between spirits, to another the ability to speak in different kinds of tongues, and to still another the interpretation of tongues. All these are the work of one and the same Spirit, and he gives them to each one, just as he determines.—1 Cor 12:4-11

The gifts are different, but the responsibility of using them is the same in every case. And yet notice the conduct of these servants.

The man who had received the five talents went at once and put his money to work and gained five more. So also, the one with the two talents gained two more. But the man who had received the one talent went off, dug a hole in the ground and hid his master's money.—Mt 25:16-18

Two of the servants used their talents faithfully; but one of them thought his talent was so small that it would not amount to anything much, even if he did use it, and the risk of failure seemed to him too great. Therefore he hid it in a safe place, to be returned intact to the Master when he should call for an account.

"After a long time the master of those servants returned and settled accounts with them. The man who had received the five talents brought the other five. 'Master,' he said, 'you entrusted me with five talents. See, I have gained five more.' . . .

"Then the man who had received the one talent came. 'Master,' he said, 'I knew that you are a hard man, harvesting where you have not sown and gathering where you have not scattered seed. So I was afraid and went out and hid your talent in the ground. See, here is what belongs to you.'"—Mt 25:19-22, 24-25

There are many such Christians in the household of faith. They are conscious of possessing only one talent, and that, perhaps, a very insignificant one; and they cannot see that any good whatever can possibly come from the using of it. Then, besides, they have hard thoughts of their Divine Master, and believe that his judgment of them and of their work will be as critical and severe, as they fear human judgments will be, or as their own have often been of others, and consequently they are afraid to work at all.

> You speak continually against your brother / and slander your own mother's son. / These things you have done and I kept silent; / you thought I was altogether like you. / But I will rebuke you / and accuse you to your face.—Ps 50:20-21

Many sit and judge their brother harshly, and then they think God is like themselves, and will judge them as harshly; and they are afraid of him, as though he were a "hard man."

> "Then another servant came and said, 'Sir, here is your mina; I have kept it laid away in a piece of cloth. I was afraid of you, because you are a hard man. You take out what you did not put in and reap what you did not sow.'"—Lk 19:20-21

We are far too apt to think that God is "altogether like us" in the worst elements of our characters, and to doubt whether he is as good as ourselves in the best.

We think his judgments are as harsh and exacting as ours often are; but we never dream his love is as charitable, and considerate, and tender as ours sometimes is. If we would judge him by our best instead of by our worst, we would form a far different idea of him, and be far less afraid of him, than is now, alas, too often the case.

Contrast the final judgment given in the case of these servants. To the one with five talents was said:

> "His master replied, 'Well done, good and faithful servant! You have been faithful with a few things; I will put you in charge of many things. Come and share your master's happiness!'"
> —Mt 25:21

To the one with two talents was said:

> "His master replied, 'Well done, good and faithful servant! You have been faithful with a few things; I will put you in charge of many things. Come and share your master's happiness!'"
>
> —Mt 25:23

To the one with one talent was said:

> "His master replied, 'You wicked, lazy servant! So you knew that I harvest where I have not sown and gather where I have not scattered seed? Well then, you should have put my money on deposit with the bankers, so that when I returned I would have received it back with interest.
>
> "'Take the talent from him and give it to the one who has the ten talents. For everyone who has will be given more, and he will have an abundance. Whoever does not have, even what he has will be taken from him.—Mt 25:26-29

In the two first cases it is "Well done, good and faithful servant," and in the last, "you wicked, lazy servant." The difference was not in the *amount* done or left undone, but in the faithfulness or unfaithfulness to the talents given. The servant with the two talents was commended in just the same words as the one with five. And the servant with only one talent, would have received a similar approval, had he shown a similar faithfulness.

For *such* a commendation who would not strive? To hear the Master say, "Well done" at last, would surely repay one for all that might have been passed through to deserve it!

> So then, men ought to regard us as servants of Christ and as those entrusted with the secret things of God.—1 Cor 4:1-2

> Whoever can be trusted with very little can also be trusted with much, and whoever is dishonest with very little will also be dishonest with much.—Lk 16:10

A servant is not responsible for the *amount* of things entrusted to his care. He is only responsible for the care of that which is entrusted; and the praise or blame that awaits him depends altogether and only upon the way he has fulfilled his trust, whether that trust has been one talent or many.

Alas! how many talents are "laid away in a piece of cloth" in the church of Christ, whose owners never dream of the sad condemnation that awaits them! Their sole duty was to put the talent to work, but because it was small and apparently of little account, they have failed. We are not praised or blamed for the number of our talents, but simply and only for the faithful or unfaithful use of those given. We cannot escape this fact. One day we must face our record in reference to it; and far better will it be for us to do this now, than to wait until it is too late to alter it.

> For we must all appear before the judgment seat of Christ, that each one may receive what is due him for the things done while in the body, whether good or bad.—2 Cor 5:10

> For God will bring every deed into judgment, / including every hidden thing, / whether it is good or evil.—Eccl 12:14

> So then, each of us will give an account of himself to God.
> —Rom 14:12

We cannot avoid giving this "account," for it is one that gives itself. Our life work tells in the formation of character, and it is the character we have formed that is to be the judgment given. In the very nature of things we receive according to what we have done, and we cannot help it.

> "And throw that worthless servant outside, into the darkness, where there will be weeping and gnashing of teeth."—Mt 25:30

This is a very solemn word. For we see that it is the "worthless servant" merely, who was cast into this outer darkness where there is weeping and gnashing of teeth: not one who had committed some great crime, but one who had simply been unprofitable. And it was a "servant" too; not an outsider, but one of the "household," evidently a believer in his Lord and Master. Have we ever dreamed that to be merely a "worthless servant" was so serious and grievous a thing as this?

We Christians have been used to appropriating this Scripture to sinners, feeling that, as for ourselves, we had nothing to do with it, and need not give it a second thought. But we cannot escape this fact, that it was a condemnation pronounced on the unprofitable servant, who had done nothing but hide his talent in the earth because he was afraid to use it. I would that every child of God would solemnly consider this.

But some may think that they at least do not possess even the one talent. The remainder of our chapter will answer such.

Our Lord at once followed the parable we have been considering, with another, which was evidently intended to elucidate the first, and to show what *is* the work he has given us to do, and what *are* the talents, whether one or many, which he has bestowed upon us.

> When the Son of Man comes in his glory, and all the angels with him, he will sit on his throne in heavenly glory. All the nations will be gathered before him, and he will separate the people one from another as a shepherd separates the sheep from the goats. He will put the sheep on his right and the goats on his left.
>
> Then the King will say to those on his right, "Come, you who are blessed by my Father; take your inheritance, the kingdom prepared for you since the creation of the world. For I was hungry and you gave me something to eat, I was thirsty and you gave me something to drink, I was a stranger and you invited me in, I needed clothes and you clothed me, I was sick and you looked after me, I was in prison and you came to visit me." ...
>
> Then he will say to those on his left, "Depart from me, you who are cursed, into the eternal fire prepared for the devil and his angels. For I was hungry and you gave me nothing to eat, I was thirsty and you gave me nothing to drink, I was a stranger and you did not invite me in, I needed clothes and you did not clothe me, I was sick and in prison and you did not look after me."
>
> —Mt 25:31-36, 41-43

The work to which we are called is the Christlike work of helping and saving, and the talents given us for use are those common to humanity, i.e., the power of ministering to the sick, and helpless, and needy, and sinful. The difference between the sheep and the goats was just this, that the one put these homely talents to Christ-like work, and the other did not.

Religion that God our Father accepts as pure and faultless is this: to look after orphans and widows in their distress and to keep oneself from being polluted by the world.—Jas 1:27

What good is it, my brothers, if a man claims to have faith but has no deeds? Can such faith save him? Suppose a brother or sister is without clothes and daily food. If one of you says to him, "go I wish you well; keep warm and well fed," but does nothing about his physical needs, what good is it? In the same way, faith by itself, if it is not accompanied by action, is dead.

But someone will say, "You have faith; I have deeds."
—Jas 2:14-18

It is always easy to *say* things, but the *doing* is the vital point. It is possible to be very "pious" in all religious performances, to fast and pray and "say" all manner of good things; and yet to have after all very little "religion that God our Father accepts as pure and faultless"; and to be, without knowing it, classed in the mind of the Master among the goats on his left hand at the last.

"Why have we fasted," they say, / "and you have not seen it? / Why have we humbled ourselves, / and you have not noticed?" / Yet on the day of your fasting, you do as you please / and exploit all your workers. / Your fasting ends in quarreling and strife, / and in striking each other with wicked fists. / You cannot fast as you do today / and expect your voice to be heard on high. / Is this the kind of fast I have chosen, / only a day for a man to humble himself? / Is it only for bowing one's head like a reed / and for lying on sackcloth and ashes? / Is that what you call a fast, / a day acceptable to the Lord? / "Is not this the kind of fasting I have chosen: to loose the chains of injustice / and untie the cords of the yoke, / to set the oppressed free / and break every yoke? / Is it not to share your food with the hungry / and to provide the poor wanderer with shelter— / when you see the naked, to clothe him, / and not to turn away from your own flesh and blood?—Is 58:3-7

All the talking, or fasting, or weeping, or wearing of sackcloth in the world, will not do as a substitute for the Christ-like life of love and kindness towards our fellow-men. The "fast he has chosen" is to help the needy and raise the fallen, and nothing will do instead of this.

A great many Christians never do anything except "for themselves." Whether they fast, or whether they eat and drink, it is all for themselves, to save their own souls, or to help forward their own experience; but they never lift a hand to help anyone else. Their religion is all for self-exaltation, in one way or another, either now or hereafter, and not truly for the glory of God at all. And they are so absorbed in self, that they do not even know that they are condemned.

> They also will answer, "Lord, when did we see you hungry or thirsty or a stranger or needing clothes or sick or in prison, and did not help you?"
> He will reply, "I tell you the truth, whatever you did not do for one of the least of these, you did not do for me."—Mt 25:44-45

"When did we see you" they ask; never dreaming that because they have not served their fellow men, they have therefore failed to serve their Master.

> Then they will go away to eternal punishment, but the righteous to eternal life.—Mt 25:46

Notice the grievous condemnation here bestowed upon those who had simply failed to do this Christ-like work. The punishment inflicted is not because of actual sins committed, but simply and only because of some kind deeds left undone. And I fear lest some church members, who have been very lavish in meting out this condemnation to the outside sinner, may find that it belongs quite as much to themselves, viewed in the searching light of God's eternal day.

> By their fruit you will recognize them. Do people pick grapes from thornbushes, or figs from thistles? Likewise every good tree bears good fruit, but a bad tree bears bad fruit. A good tree cannot

bear bad fruit, and a bad tree cannot bear good fruit. Every tree that does not bear good fruit is cut down and thrown into the fire. Thus, by their fruit you will recognize them.

Not everyone who says to me, "Lord, Lord," will enter the kingdom of heaven, but only he who does the will of my Father who is in heaven. Many will say to me on that day, "Lord, Lord, did we not prophesy in your name, and in your name drive out demons and perform many miracles?" Then I will tell them plainly, "I never knew you. Away from me, you evildoers!"
—Mt 7:16-23 (Mt 25:37-40)

When we put forth our hands to help any soul for whom Christ died, even though that soul may have been so sinful as to be cast into prison, we are doing it to him. Let these blessed words "Inasmuch" and "Well done" fire our souls to all deeds of kindness and of love.

"Teacher," said John, "we saw a man driving out demons in your name and we told him to stop, because he was not one of us."

"Do not stop him," Jesus said. "No one who does a miracle in my name can in the next moment say anything bad about me, for whoever is not against us is for us. I tell you the truth, anyone who gives you a cup of water in my name because you belong to Christ will certainly not lose his reward."—Mk 9:38-41

All Christ-like work is begotten by Christ, even though it may be by one who is not "one of us." Christ was goodness personified, and he who is good is allied to Christ although he may never have heard of him. Whoever takes the side of goodness, takes the side of Christ, in the mind of God. It is as if a lone man, in the midst of slave-holders, should come to a belief in freedom for slaves. We would say of him, "he is one of us"; although he might never have heard of the group to which we belong. Surely we could never forbid such a one either by word or deed from casting out the devils of sin and oppression, nor refuse to join in his work.

Not even so small a talent as a cup of water, is too small to be used for the Master; and to this, equally as to the great hospital built or the great reform wrought by those of larger gifts, will the blessed approval come, "Well done, good and faithful servant." And perhaps even more to the first than to the last.

Jesus sat down opposite the place where the offerings were put and watched the crowd putting their money into the temple treasury. Many rich people threw in large amounts. But a poor widow came and put in two very small copper coins, worth only a fraction of a penny.

Calling his disciples to him, Jesus said, "I tell you the truth, this poor widow has put more into the treasury than all the others. They all gave out of their wealth; but she, out of her poverty, put in everything—all she had to live on."—Mk 12:41-44

It is not much to give out of one's abundance; but to give "out of one's poverty," all that one has, whether in time, or in talent, or in sympathy, this is the thing that receives the Lord's approval. If then you have only one talent, and the service you render is "out of your poverty" instead of out of your abundance, even though it be all that you have, cast it into the Lord's treasury, and be sure you shall win his approval, whether the world approves or not.

In Exodus 35 we have a beautiful picture of the sort of service our divine Master loves. Each one brought *what he had*. And they brought it so willingly, that soon there was more than enough.

All who were willing, men and women alike, came and brought gold jewelry of all kinds; brooches, earrings, rings and ornaments. . . . All the Israelite men and women who were willing brought to the Lord freewill offerings for all the work the Lord through Moses had commanded them to do.
—Ex 35:22, 29 (Ex 25:22-28; Ex 36:3-7)

If this sort of service were offered by the church of Christ to her divine Master now, it would not be so hard as it is to find willing workers to send forth into the great harvest field.

Remember this: Whoever sows sparingly will also reap sparingly, and whoever sows generously will also reap generously.

Each man should give what he has decided in his heart to give, not reluctantly or under compulsion, for God loves a cheerful giver.
—2 Cor 9:6-7

"Willing" service is the only kind that is really acceptable to the Lord. We are apt to think that the service which is a "cross" to us must be more meritorious. But is it more meritorious for a mother and father to care for their children if they find it a "great cross" to do so? Do we value the services of our friends more, if they are grudging services, than if they are poured out willingly from loving hearts? And can we imagine our divine Master will feel about service to himself differently from us?

The king's officials answered him, "Your servants are ready to do whatever our lord the king chooses." —2 Sm 15:15

"Whatever," let it be one talent or five; *my* work, not the work of any other, a cup of water, a mite, a few kind words, a murmured prayer, "whatever" your hands find to do, do it with your might. And your reward shall be sure. For whether your talents be five or one, if they are only faithfully used for the Master, there shall certainly one day sound in thy ears the blessed words, "Well done."

Be dressed ready for service and keep your lamps burning, like men waiting for their master to return from a wedding banquet, so that when he comes and knocks they can immediately open the door for him. It will be good for those servants whose master finds them watching when he comes. I tell you the truth, he will dress himself to serve, will have them recline at the table and will come and wait on them. It will be good for those servants whose master finds them ready, even if he comes in the second or third watch of the night. But understand this: If the owner of the house had known at what hour the thief was coming, he would not have let his house be broken into. You also must be ready, because the Son of Man will come at an hour when you do not expect him."
—Lk 12:35-40

Let us close our lesson then with the solemn question asked

by David of the children of Israel, hundreds of years ago; and let us make our answer as full and prompt as theirs.

And who then is willing to consecrate his *service* this day unto the Lord.—1 Chr 29:5KJV (1 Chr 29:6-9)

TWELVE

God Owns Us

Foundation Text— *Do you not know that your body is a temple of the Holy Spirit, who is in you, whom you have received from God? You are not your own; you were bought at a price. Therefore honor God with your body.* —1 Cor 6:19-20

"Do you not know? Alas! how few of us really *know* that we are not our own, and that we do actually and truly belong to God! We have heard it and read of it often enough, and have perhaps thought we believed it; but as to really *knowing* it, this is a different matter. And yet it is essential to our peace and well being that we should know it. Any doubt as to our real place and position toward God is a grievous hindrance to our spiritual prosperity and development.

Hear, O heavens! Listen, O earth! / For the Lord has spoken: / "I reared children and brought them up, / but they have rebelled against me. / The ox knows his master, / the donkey his owner's manager, / but Israel does not know, / my people do not understand."—Is 1:2-3

My people are destroyed from lack of knowledge. / "Because you have rejected knowledge, / I also reject you as my priests; / because you have ignored the law of your God, / I also will ignore your children.—Hos 4:6

It is therefore of vital importance that we should know how matters stand between ourselves and the Lord. There is a great deal of hope and a great deal of desire, but knowledge after all is the only stable thing. Our first step therefore in this matter of God's ownership must be to find out the facts of the case, as to whom we really do belong, whether to ourselves or to God. Let us see what the testimony of scripture is on this.

> For every living soul belongs to me, the father as well as the son—both alike belong to me.—Ez 18:4

> For the Lord's portion is his people, / Jacob his allotted inheritance.—Dt 32:9

> If we live, we live to the Lord; and if we die, we die to the Lord. So, whether we live or die, we belong to the Lord.—Rom 14:8

We belong to God by creation; and we belong to him also in a still deeper sense by redemption.

> Yet, O Lord, you are our Father. / We are the clay, you are the potter; / we are all the work of your hand.
> —Is 64:8 (Ps 95:6-7; 100:3)

Anything a man makes is surely his own, without a possibility of question. Therefore the blessed fact that God is our Maker, involves in the very nature of things, the still more blessed fact that he is therefore our Owner also.

> But now, this is what the Lord says— / he who created you, O Jacob, / he who formed you, O Israel: / "Fear not, for I have redeemed you; / I have called you by name; you are mine.—Is 43:1

In a still deeper sense is God our owner, because he has redeemed us. All the world over, the rights of a man's possession, in anything he has bought and paid for, are recognized without a question; and if we apply this rule to the fact that *we* have been purchased by the "precious blood of Christ," we shall get a little idea of how utterly and incontrovertibly we belong to him.

> For you know that it was not with perishable things such as silver or gold that you were redeemed from the empty way of life handed

down to you from your forefathers, but with the precious blood of Christ, a lamb without blemish or defect.—1 Pt 1:18-19

Husbands, love your wives, just as Christ loved the church and gave himself up for her.—Eph 5:25 (Acts 20:28)

He "gave himself for us." Could he have paid a greater price than this?

> Love divine! of such great loving,
>   Only mothers know the cost;
> Cost of love, that, all love passing,
>   Gave itself to save the lost.

Just as the Father knows me and I know the Father—and I lay down my life for the sheep.—Jn 10:15

You see, at just the right time, when we were still powerless, Christ died for the ungodly. Very rarely will anyone die for a righteous man, though for a good man someone might possibly dare to die. But God demonstrates his own love for us in this: While we were still sinners, Christ died for us.—Rom 5:6-8

But just here we must avoid the mistake of thinking that redemption was a price paid *to* God, as to an angry creditor. It was a price paid *for* sin, the price that love always must pay for the sin of those whom it loves. We are "bought with a price," and, because of this, we belong body, soul, and spirit to the One who has bought us.

> The kingdom of heaven is like treasure hidden in a field. When a man found it, he hid it again, and then in his joy went and sold all he had and bought that field.
> Again, the kingdom of heaven is like a merchant looking for fine pearls. When he found one of great value, he went away and sold everything he had and bought it.—Mt 13:44-46

Christ sold "all he had" to purchase the "field," which is the world, for the sake of the "treasure" that is hidden there, which is humanity. (This is not the usual interpretation of the passage, but by comparing Christ's own words, "the field is the world," in Matthew 13:38, I think we will find it admissible.)

And again, the pearl of great price may also be considered to be the human race whom Christ purchased with his own blood, "all he had."

Surely, after all this, we cannot question the fact of his ownership!

Since, then, it is a settled fact that we are not our own, but that we belong to God, let us consider what follows from this.

1. His ownership of us lays upon him the responsibility of caring for us.

2. It lays upon us the responsibility of surrender, and trust, and obedience to him.

We will consider first the responsibilities of ownership.

If anyone does not provide for his relatives, and especially for his immediate family, he has denied the faith and is worse than an unbeliever.—1 Tm 5:8

The whole world acknowledges the justice of this. To own anything means that the owner is bound to care for and protect and bless, to the limit of ability, that which is owned. We are all accustomed to looking so exclusively on the human side of the question of our salvation, on *our* duties and *our* responsibilities, that we lose sight almost altogether of God's side, and thus miss of that, which after all, is the vital point of the whole matter. The responsibilities of an owner, and much more of a Creator, are greater than can be expressed. Parents feel this, and by a universal instinct, which is inalienable in our natures, all parents are held responsible to their own consciences and to their fellow-men for the welfare of their children. In the same way, owners of animals, or owners of property, or owners of anything whatever, are considered to be bound to care for that which they own, and are held responsible for its welfare. Even children feel this responsibility, and will fulfil the duties of ownership, no matter how irksome, feeding the bird or the rabbit without complaint because it is their own.

In Mary Shelley's *Frankenstein* we have an allegory that vividly illustrates this truth. The writer imagines a student who has penetrated into the secrets of life, and who proposes to make a man. He spends some two years in framing a huge being, creating bones and muscle and tendons and nerves, and arranging them in their relative order. At the proper moment he communicates the vital spark, and the creature opens its eyes, stares around it, and begins to move. The workman is suddenly awakened to a sense of the awful responsibility he has incurred in the act of creation, and flies in terror from the work of his hands. But he cannot escape his responsibilities. The creature wanders over the earth, making misery for itself and others wherever it goes, and its creator is forced to follow it in order to atone for its mistakes and its sins, and to free it from its continually recurring difficulties. At last they have an interview, and the creature reproaches the man for having made it, and tells him that he is responsible for all that it has done and suffered.

Our Lord himself asserts this truth when he compares himself and his own faithful care of his sheep, to the neglect and unfaithfulness of a hired hand "who does not own the sheep."

> I am the good shepherd. The good shepherd lays down his life for the sheep. The hired hand is not the shepherd who owns the sheep. So when he sees the wolf coming, he abandons the sheep and runs away. Then the wolf attacks the flock and scatters it. The man runs away because he is a hired hand and cares nothing for the sheep.
> I am the good shepherd; I know my sheep and my sheep know me.—Jn 10:11-14

In Ezekiel we have a vivid description of the stern disapproval with which the Lord regards those shepherds who care for themselves rather than for the flocks under their control.

> The word of the Lord came to me: "Son of man, prophesy against the shepherds of Israel; prophesy and say to them: 'This is

what the Sovereign Lord says: Woe to the shepherds of Israel who only take care of themselves! Should not shepherds take care of the flock? You eat the curds, clothe yourselves with the wool and slaughter the choice animals, but you do not take care of the flock. You have not strengthened the weak or healed the sick or bound up the injured. You have not brought back the strays or searched for the lost. You have ruled them harshly and brutally.
—Ez 34:1-4 (Ez 34:5-10; Jer 23:1-2; Zc 11:17)

From these condemnations of the idle shepherds who do not own the sheep we may learn what the duties of the owner of the sheep must be. These foolish shepherds fed themselves but not the flock; the owner would feed the flock, even though he must go without himself. These false shepherds neglected the diseased, and failed to strengthen the weak, they did not seek for those who were lost and they ruled the flock "harshly and brutally"; the owner heals the sick, and strengthens the weak, and seeks the lost, and rules the flock with gentleness and love.

For this is what the Sovereign Lord says: I myself will search for my sheep and look after them. As a shepherd looks after his scattered flock when he is with them, so will I look after my sheep. I will rescue them from all the places where they were scattered on a day of clouds and darkness. . . . I myself will tend my sheep and have them lie down, declares the Sovereign Lord. I will search for the lost and bring back the strays. I will bind up the injured and strengthen the weak, but the sleek and the strong I will destroy. I will shepherd the flock with justice.—Ez 34:11-12, 15-16

And such is Christ, the "Good Shepherd," to whom the sheep belong.

The scroll of the prophet Isaiah was handed to him. Unrolling it, he found the place where it is written: / "The Spirit of the Lord is on me, / because he has anointed me / to preach good news to the poor. / He has sent me to proclaim freedom for the prisoners / and recovery of sight for the blind, / to release the oppressed, / to proclaim the year of the Lord's favor." / Then he rolled up the scroll, gave it back to the attendant and sat down. The eyes of everyone in the synagogue were fastened on him, and he began by saying to them, "Today this scripture is fulfilled in your hearing."—Lk 4:17-21

In all ages of the church this responsibility of ownership has been recognized. Moses referred to it as being a burden greater than he could bear, and reminded the Lord that because the Israelites were *his* people, therefore the care of them must rest upon *his* shoulders and not upon Moses' own shoulders. Had they belonged to Moses, it would have been his duty to care for them; but since they belonged to God it was plainly God's duty.

> He asked the Lord, "Why have you brought this trouble on your servant? What have I done to displease you that you put the burden of all these people on me? Did I conceive all these people? Did I give them birth? Why do you tell me to carry them in my arms, as a nurse carries an infant, to the land you promised on oath to their forefathers? Where can I get meat for all these people? They keep wailing to me, 'Give us meat to eat!' I cannot carry all these people by myself; the burden is too heavy for me.
> —Nm 11:11-14

> And forgive your people, who have sinned against you; forgive all the offenses they have committed against you, and cause their conquerors to show them mercy; for they are your people and your inheritance, whom you brought out of Egypt, out of that iron smelting furnace.—1 Kg 8:50 (Dt 9:27-29)

"For they are your people"; this was a plea that admitted of no denial. Nehemiah and Isaiah realized this, and made similar pleas.

> They are your servants and your people, whom you redeemed by your great strength and your mighty hand. O Lord, let your ear be attentive to the prayer of this your servant and to the prayer of your servants who delight in revering your name. Give your servant success today by granting him favor in the presence of this man." I was cupbearer to the king.—Neh 1:10-11

> Yet, O Lord, you are our Father. / We are the clay, you are the potter; / we are all the work of your hand. / Do not be angry

beyond measure, O Lord; / do not remember our sins forever. / Oh, look upon us, we pray, / for we are all your people.—Is 64:8-9

"For we are all your people!" Where could we find a stronger plea?

The responsibility of ownership is an inexorable divine law, which is only another name for the eternal nature of things. And if we can realize this, it will make the fact of our being owned by God one of the most comforting and peace-giving facts in existence.

But now, this is what the Lord says— / he who created you, O Jacob, / he who formed you, O Israel: / "Fear not, for I have redeemed you; / I have called you by name; you are mine. / When you pass through the waters, / I will be with you; / and when you pass through the rivers, / they will not sweep over you. / When you walk through the fire, / you will not be burned; / the flames will not set you ablaze. / For I am the Lord, your God, / the Holy One of Israel, your Savior; / I give Egypt for your ransom, / Cush and Seba in your stead. / Since you are precious and honored in my sight, / and because I love you, / I will give men in exchange for you, / and people in exchange for your life. / Do not be afraid, for I am with you; / I will bring your children from the east / and gather you from the west. / I will say to the north, 'Give them up!' / and to the south, 'Do not hold them back.' / Bring my sons from afar / and my daughters from the ends of the earth— / everyone who is called by my name, / whom I created for my glory, / whom I formed and made."—Is 43:1-7

All this therefore, and infinitely more, will the Lord do for us because he has made us and we belong to him. Can we feel anything but joy then to know that we are his? I remember when the bliss of this divine ownership first dawned upon my soul. I was in the woods away from man's world, almost alone in God's world of nature. I was reading the verse, "You are not your own, you are bought with a price," when suddenly the veil parted and I saw what it meant. No words could tell what that sight was! But I had to hold my Bible open and keep my finger on the printed verse to make myself sure that the bliss that had dawned upon me could really be true. And from that moment, to belong to God has seemed to me the blessing of all blessings in my life!

To the soul that has had a revelation such as this, it can never be anything but joy to sing the good old hymn:

Lord, I am thine, entirely thine,
Purchased and saved by love divine;
With full consent thine will I be,
And own thy sovereign right in me.

Sometimes the fact of God's "sovereign right" in us is looked upon as a hard thing, and the soul shrinks and hesitates from consenting to it. But that can only be because such a one does not know what it means.

Let us consider more fully what it is that he does for his own.

1. He loves his own.

It was just before the Passover Feast. Jesus knew that the time had come for him to leave this world and go to the Father. Having loved his own who were in the world, he now showed them the full extent of his love.—Jn 13:1

2. He lays down his life for his own.

I am the good shepherd. The good shepherd lays down his life for the sheep.—Jn 10:11 (Eph 5:2)

3. He seeks his own when they are lost.

The Son of Man came to save what was lost.

What do you think? If a man owns a hundred sheep, and one of them wanders away, will he not leave the ninety-nine on the hills and go to look for the one that wandered off?—Mt 18:11-13

4. He heals his own when they are sick.

When evening came, many who were demon-possessed were brought to him, and he drove out the spirits with a word and healed all the sick. This was to fulfill what was spoken through the prophet Isaiah:

"He took up our infirmities / and carried our diseases."
—Mt 8:16-17

5. He strengthens his own when they are weak.

But he said to me, "My grace is sufficient for you, for my power is made perfect in weakness." Therefore I will boast all the more gladly about my weaknesses, so that Christ's power may rest on me.—2 Cor 12:9

6. He delivers his own from their enemies.

For he will deliver the needy who cry out,
the afflicted who have no one to help.—Ps 72:12

7. He keeps his own from danger.

I, the Lord, watch over it; / I water it continually. / I guard it day and night / so that no one may harm it.—Is 27:3

8. He leads and teaches his own.

This is what the Lord says— / your Redeemer, the Holy One of Israel: / "I am the Lord your God, / who teaches you what is best for you, / who directs you in the way you should go."—Is 48:17

9. He supplies all their needs.

And my God will meet all your needs according to his glorious riches in Christ Jesus.—Phil 4:19

10. He carries all their cares.

Cast all your anxiety on him because he cares for you.—1 Pt 5:7

Cast your cares on the Lord / and he will sustain you; / he will never let the righteous fall.—Ps 55:22

11. He purifies his own.

Who gave himself for us to redeem us from all wickedness and to purify for himself a people that are his very own, eager to do what is good.—Ti 2:14

12. He gives his own all things.

So then, no more boasting about men! All things are yours, whether Paul or Apollos or Cephas or the world or life or death or the present or the future—all are yours, and you are of Christ, and Christ is of God.—1 Cor 3:21-23

13. He makes his own one with himself, and gives them a share in his glory.

My prayer is not for them alone. I pray also for those who will believe in me through their message, that all of them may be one, Father, just as you are in me and I am in you. May they also be in us so that the world may believe that you have sent me.
—Jn 17:20-22 (Jn 17:23-24)

In the face of such revelations as these, who would not be eager to surrender themselves to such a blessed ownership and control? The control of love is always lovely, even when that love is earthly; because in the very nature of things love *can* choose only the best it knows for its beloved ones, and *must* pour itself out to the last drop to help and to bless them. How much more then must be the blessedness of the control of God, who is love; who is not merely loving, but is Love itself, and in whose ownership there must be and can be nothing but infinite and fathomless bliss!

Our views are so limited and our thoughts are so bounded by self, that we are apt to think far more of the fact that the Lord belongs to us, than that we belong to him. But when we come to consider it, we can see in a moment how much more vital and full of blessing is God's ownership of us, than ours of him could ever possibly be. If *we* own him, then the responsibility of keeping him is upon our shoulders. While if *he* owns us, this responsibility is on his shoulders. Moreover our keeping is such a poor thing, that if it depended on us we should be sure to lose him, while we can never have any fear of him losing us.

The soul does not always find this out at once. It is a knowledge that comes with spiritual growth. In the Song of Songs there are three passages that develop this growing knowledge.

The soul thinks first of its own ownership of its Beloved, and ranks his ownership of herself in the second place.

> My lover is mine and I am his; / he browses among the lilies.
> —Sg 2:16

The soul learns next that the Lord's ownership is the most important, and must take the first place.

> I am my lover's and my lover is mine; / he browses among the lilies.—Sg 6:3

The soul learns at last that the only important thing is his ownership, and forgets to mention her own at all.

> I belong to my lover, / and his desire is for me.—Sg 7:10

The question next arises as to what are the responsibilities that rest upon us in view of the fact that God's owns us. They are very simple. We are only responsible to do three things: to yield, to trust, to obey. We *are* the Lord's; now we must recognize this, and must acknowledge him as our Owner and Master, and must abandon ourselves to his care and control.

> Therefore, I urge you, brothers, in view of God's mercy, to offer your bodies as living sacrifices, holy and pleasing to God—which is your spiritual worship.—Rom 12:1

It is indeed only a "reasonable service," for those who are in the Lord's blessed ownership, to consent to it, and consciously and intelligently give themselves up to his control. A man's "own possessions" are either a credit to him or a disgrace; and we cannot be a credit to our Lord and Master unless we submit ourselves to him, and let him have his own way with us.

> ... You were bought with a price. Therefore honor God with your body.—1 Cor 6:20 (Is 43:21; Eph 1:12)

> ... "So I bound the whole house of Israel and the whole house of Judah to me" declares the Lord, "To be my people for my renown and praise and honor. But they have not listened."—Jer 13:11

May it never be said of any of us that we "would not hear!"

> But you his son, O Belshazzar, have not humbled yourself, though you knew all this. Instead, you have set yourself up against the Lord of heaven. You had the goblets from his temple brought to you, and you and your nobles, your wives and your concubines drank wine from them. You praised the gods of silver and gold, of bronze, iron, wood and stone, which cannot see or hear or understand. But you did not honor the God who holds in his hand your life and all your ways.—Dn 5:22-23

Since we are not our own, we must not "live for ourselves," and we can therefore have no liberty to use ourselves for our own purposes.

> And he died for all, that those who live should no longer live for themselves but for him who died for them and was raised again.
> 2 Cor 5:15 (1 Pt 4:1-2)

Further since we belong to the Lord, we must let the world see how well he cares for us, by receiving in childlike faith all the good things he would bestow upon us.

> Nevertheless, I will bring health and healing to it; I will heal my people and will let them enjoy abundant peace and security. I will bring Judah and Israel back from captivity and will rebuild them as they were before. I will cleanse them from all the sin they have committed against me and will forgive all their sins of rebellion against me. Then this city will bring me renown, joy, praise and honor before all nations on earth that hear of all the good things I do for it; and they will be in awe and will tremble at the abundant prosperity and peace I provide for it.—Jer 33:6-9

Contrast with this the dishonor that Moses felt would come upon the Lord, should the Israelites fail in receiving the promised deliverance.

> If you put these people to death all at one time, the nations who have heard this report about you will say, "The Lord was not able to bring these people into the land he promised them on oath; so he slaughtered them in the desert. —Nm 14:15-16 (Nm 14:13-14)

Let us then show, by the thoroughness of our trust in him, the utter trustworthiness of the Lord "whose we are and whom we serve"; and let us allow him to save us to the very uttermost, lest the world should say (as, alas, they already do) that it is because "the Lord is not able."

What is needed therefore is that we should first come into a clear knowledge of God's ownership, and then that we should "live up" to this knowledge. There are certain definite exercises of soul that will help the heart into this knowledge. These are set forth in Deuteronomy 26.

> And say to the priest in office at the time, "I declare today to the Lord your God that I have come to the land the Lord swore to our forefathers to give us." . . . He brought us to this place and gave us this land, a land flowing with milk and honey." . . . You have declared this day that the Lord is your God and that you will walk in his ways, that you will keep his decrees, commands and laws, and that you will obey him. And the Lord has declared this day that you are his people, his treasured possession as he promised, and that you are to keep all his commands. He has declared that he will set you in praise, fame and honor high above all the nations he has made and that you will be a people holy to the Lord your God, as he promises. —Dt 26:3, 9, 17-19

First, we must confess that God owns us. "I declare today to the Lord your God that I have come to the land" (verse 3), and, "He brought us to this place, and had given us this land" (verse 9). Then we must declare the Lord to be our God, and must surrender ourselves to his control (verse 17). And then finally we shall know that the Lord declares us to be his people, as he has promised us (verse 18). And the question of our foundation text, "Do you not know that your body is a temple of the Holy Spirit?... You are not your own" will be answered with a glad and hearty "Yes, I do know it! I am not my own, but God's. I belong to him alone, and he is my sole and sovereign Owner."

> Since I belong to thee, my Savior, God,
> All must be well, however rough my road;
> However dark my way or prospects be,
> All, all is right, since overruled by thee.
>
> Feeblest of all thy flock, thou knowest me, Lord;
> Helpless and weak, I stay upon thy word;
> In all my weakness, this is still my plea,
> That thou art mine, and I belong to thee.
>
> Then come whatever may, I am secure,
> Thy love unchanged shall to the end endure;
> Frail though I am, thine everlasting arm
> Shall shield thy child from every breath of harm.

THIRTEEN

The Resurrection Life of the Believer

Foundation Text— *We were therefore buried with him through baptism into death in order that, just as Christ was raised from the dead through the glory of the Father, we too may live a new life.* —Rom 6:4

Notice the "we too" of this passage. It surely teaches that the life we are called to live here and now is something of the same nature as the life Christ was to live when he was raised from the dead. It is a life belonging to the same order of things, an *interior* resurrection life, to be lived here in these earthly bodies.

> We always carry around in our body the death of Jesus, so that the life of Jesus may also be revealed in our body. For we who are alive are always being given over to death for Jesus' sake, so that his life may be revealed in our mortal body.—2 Cor 4:10-11

> Having been buried with him in baptism and raised with him through your faith in the power of God, who raised him from the dead.
> When you were dead in your sins and in the uncircumcision of your sinful nature, God made you alive with Christ. He forgave us all our sins.—Col 2:12-13

It is just as though one had died and been buried, and had risen again, and thenceforth walked in a new and risen life. Such a one would look at things from an altogether different standpoint, and measure them by other measures. Try to put yourself in the place of Lazarus after he had been raised from the dead, and imagine, if you can, with what eyes he would behold the world and the things of it; and you will perhaps get a glimpse of the meaning of this resurrection life. Things once all-important to him, must have lost their value, and things once insignificant, must have become of mighty import.

> But because of his great love for us, God, who is rich in mercy, made us alive with Christ even when we were dead in transgressions—it is by grace you have been saved. And God raised us up with Christ and seated us with him in the heavenly realms in Christ Jesus.—Eph 2:4-6

The place from which we look, makes all the difference in the aspect of things. The resurrection life seats us in "heavenly places," and we look from these *down* upon earthly things, and not *up* from earthly places upon heavenly things. We are to walk through this world as those whose heart and brain move there, while our feet stay here.

Our "views" are simply what we *see,* and not necessarily what really *is.* A man at the foot of the mountain, and a man on the summit, may both look in the same direction, but their "views" would be widely different.

> I have given them your word and the world has hated them, for they are not of the world any more than I am of the world. My prayer is not that you take them out of the world but that you protect them from the evil one. They are not of the world, even as I am not of it.—Jn 17:14-16

We are "not of the world" in the sense that we belong to a spiritual race whose home is in a higher sphere, and who go through this world only as pilgrims and strangers. We belong to the heavenly order, not the earthly; and our sphere of true living is not on the material plane, but on the spiritual. As someone has said, "we are encamped in nature, but not domesticated."

> Since, then, you have been raised with Christ, set your hearts on things above, where Christ is seated at the right hand of God. Set your minds on things above, not on earthly things. For you died, and your life is now hidden with Christ in God.—Col 3:1-3

> For here we do not have an enduring city, but we are looking for the city that is to come.—Heb 13:14

We say of some men that they "grovel," and we mean that their souls dwell on earthly levels, and are interested only in earthly things. Of others we say that they "soar" far above their fellows, and we mean that their souls dwell in upper regions, and their affections are set on heavenly things. The resurrection life soars. It mounts on eagle's wings into the divine region of "the life hid with Christ in God."

> But our citizenship is in heaven. And we eagerly await a Savior from there, the Lord Jesus Christ.—Phil 3:20

Our "citizenship" is not here but in heaven. Heaven means simply the spiritual sphere of things; and to have our citizenship there means, that our real home and our real interests, and possessions, and rights are all in this sphere.

> And God raised us up with Christ and seated us with him in the heavenly realms in Christ Jesus.—Eph 2:6

> Consequently, you are no longer foreigners and aliens, but fellow citizens with God's people and members of God's household.
> —Eph 2:19

To be "fellow citizens with God's people," and members of "God's household" means to live in the resurrection life.

> All these people were still living by faith when they died. They did not receive the things promised; they only saw them and welcomed them from a distance. And they admitted that they were

aliens and strangers on earth. People who say such things show that they are looking for a country of their own. If they had been thinking of the country they had left, they would have had opportunity to return. Instead, they were longing for a better country—a heavenly one. Therefore God is not ashamed to be called their God, for he has prepared a city for them.

—Heb 11:13-16

We "look for a country." Or in other words we are a *developing* race. It is not a *place* we are seeking, but a *condition* ; that is, a new nature and a new sphere of life. As has been well said, "God is gradually developing higher forms of life out of lower; the intellectual and the spiritual out of the animal and the sensuous. There are two men in the Bible, the flesh man and the spirit man, the man of the without and the man of the within; man as an animal, and man as a spiritual being, and the last is being evolved out of the first."

Therefore we do not lose heart. Though outwardly we are wasting away, yet inwardly we are being renewed day by day.

—2 Cor 4:16

I pray that out of his glorious riches he may strengthen you with power through his Spirit in your inner being.—Eph 3:16

The resurrection life of which we are speaking, is the life of this "inner man." It is a life begotten of God, and therefore partaking of the very nature of God.

Through these he has given us his very great and precious promises, so that through them you may participate in the divine nature and escape the corruption in the world caused by evil desires.—2 Pt 1:4

We, who believe the promises, "Participate in the divine nature"; but we participate in the lower nature as well. And it is the struggle between these two natures that causes our conflicts. It is in the process of development which is going on within us, that all our sin and suffering are evolved. Whenever the lower nature in us gains the supremacy, we sin, and consequently suffer.

> So I say, live by the Spirit, and you will not gratify the desires of the sinful nature. For the sinful nature desires what is contrary to the Spirit, and the Spirit what is contrary to the sinful nature. They are in conflict with each other, so that you do not do what you want.—Gal 5:16-17

> And if I do what I do not want to do, I agree that the law is good. As it is, it is no longer I myself who do it, but it is sin living in me. . . .but I see another law at work in the members of my body, waging war against the law of my mind and making me a prisoner of the law of sin at work within my members.
> —Rom 7:16-17, 23 (Rom 7:18-22)

Our natural man, the flesh man, or as the Bible calls it, the "old man," can never fulfill the righteousness of God, for it is of the earth, earthy. With our "sinful nature," the flesh, we must necessarily always serve the "law of sin."

> Those who live according to the sinful nature have their minds set on what that nature desires; but those who live in accordance with the Spirit have their minds set on what the Spirit desires. The mind of sinful man is death, but the mind controlled by the Spirit is life and peace; the sinful mind is hostile to God. It does not submit to God's law, nor can it do so. Those controlled by the sinful nature cannot please God.—Rom 8:5-8

It is only the spiritual man, the man born of God, the resurrection man, who can mind the things of the Spirit; and in fact it is only such who can even *understand* God and his ways.

> For who among men knows the thoughts of a man except the man's spirit within him? In the same way no one knows the thoughts of God except the Spirit of God. We have not received the spirit of the world but the Spirit who is from God that we may

understand what God has freely given us. . . . "For who has known the mind of the Lord that he may instruct him?"
—1 Cor 2:11-12, 16 (1 Cor 2:13-15)

The one essential thing therefore for each one of us is to have this spiritual man, this resurrection life, born in us. Nothing avails but this. The tiger cannot understand the "thoughts of a man" because it does not have the "man's spirit" within it; and likewise we cannot understand the "thoughts of God" unless we possess the spirit of God.

Jesus answered, "I tell you the truth, unless a man is born of water and the Spirit, he cannot enter the kingdom of God. Flesh gives birth to flesh, but the Spirit gives birth to spirit. You should not be surprised at my saying, 'You must be born again.' "
—Jn 3:5-7 (Jn 3:3-4; Gal 6:15)

The new birth is a necessity in the very nature of things, for in order to enter any plane of life we must be born into it. No amount of effort can turn a tiger into a man, and no amount of effort can turn the flesh man into the spirit man. That which is born of the flesh *is* flesh, and always must be.

You, however, are controlled not by the sinful nature but by the Spirit, if the Spirit of God lives in you. And if anyone does not have the Spirit of Christ, he does not belong to Christ.—Rom 8:9

The salvation revealed by the Lord Jesus Christ, therefore, goes far deeper than the mere outward commands, "You shall," and "You shall not," which are all addressed only to that which is "born of the flesh," i.e., the natural or carnal man. The salvation of God gives man a new nature, one "born of the Spirit," that is so true and right in its very issues, as to live right outwardly without any law, from its own essential nature. The resurrection life works, not "after the law of a carnal commandment, but after the power of an endless life."

Because through Christ Jesus the law of the Spirit of life set me free from the law of sin and death. For what the law was powerless to do in that it was weakened by the sinful nature, God did by sending his own Son in the likeness of sinful man to be a sin offering. And so he condemned sin in sinful man, in order that the righteous requirements of the law might be fully met in us, who do not live according to the sinful nature but according to the Spirit.—Rom 8:2-4

It is the inward "law of the Spirit of life" that sets us free from sin; and not the outward law of ordinances. Commandments are not needed when the inward life is right.

What shall we say, then? Shall we go on sinning so that grace may increase? By no means! We died to sin; how can we live in it any longer? . . . For sin shall not be your master, because you are not under law, but under grace.
What then? Shall we sin because we are not under law but under grace? By no means!—Rom 6:1-2, 14-15 (Gal 5:18)

If a man is a thief at heart, no laws or penalties can keep him from stealing; but if a man is honest at heart, not even laws and penalties could make him steal. And this is the secret of the resurrection life. It cannot sin, because it is born of God.

If you know that he is righteous, you know that everyone who does what is right has been born of him.—1 Jn 2:29 (1 Jn 3:6-10)

This does not mean that it is impossible for a child of God to sin, but only that it is impossible for that nature in him which is born of God, to sin. Many Christians are yet to a great degree "worldly and acting like mere men."

Brothers, I could not address you as spiritual but as worldly—mere infants in Christ. I gave you milk, not solid food, for you were not yet ready for it. Indeed, you are still not ready. You are still worldly. For since there is jealousy and quarreling among you, are you not worldly? Are you not acting like mere men?
—1 Cor 3:1-3

"Infants in Christ" have the spiritual life begotten in them, but it is not yet dominant, and they are still more or less under the control of the worldly, or carnal, mind. Judged by the marks Paul gives in this passage of what the carnal mind consists in, it would seem as though not many Christians had developed out of this stage as yet!

But we *may* develop, we are meant to develop; only we do not always understand the way. We think to do it by a greater stringency of legal efforts, by stricter rules and more searching commandments. But God's way is by faith.

> Before this faith came, we were held prisoners by the law, locked up until faith should be revealed. So the law was put in charge to lead us to Christ that we might be justified by faith. Now that faith has come, we are no longer under the supervision of the law.—Gal 3:23-25

The law acts as a supervisor to bring us to Christ, but it is powerless to carry us any further, and it is only by faith that we can enter into or live the resurrection life.

> You foolish Galatians! Who has bewitched you? Before your very eyes Jesus Christ was clearly portrayed as crucified. I would like to learn just one thing from you: Did you receive the Spirit by observing the law, or by believing what you heard? Are you so foolish? After beginning with the Spirit, are you now trying to attain your goal by human effort? Have you suffered so much for nothing—if it really was for nothing? Does God give you his Spirit and work miracles among you because you observe the law, or because you believe what you heard?—Gal 3:1-4

The resurrection life is a matter of faith and development. We trust God for it, and he develops it in us.

How do people get delivered from the foolishness of childhood? Not by being commanded to give it up, but by growing out of it. When I was a child, I used to think that grown-up people wanted to play as much as I did, only there was a law against it. I thought this law came into effect at a certain age, and I pitied all the people who had reached this age, and dreaded growing old myself, because the sad time was drawing nearer for me. But when I had reached maturity, I found there was no law needed, for the desire to play was gone; I had outgrown childish things.

> When I was a child, I talked like a child, I thought like a child, I reasoned like a child. When I became a man, I put childish ways behind me.—1 Cor 13:11

And just so it is in this resurrection life. Our souls at first dread to enter upon it, because we are afraid of its demands. We want to keep our playthings, and our childish amusements. But as the divine life is developed, and the soul becomes more and more mature, it finds that the "childish ways" drop off of themselves. The resurrection life "puts them behind us" not because it *must,* but because it *wants* to, because it has outgrown them.

> Therefore, if anyone is in Christ, he is a new creation; the old has gone, the new has come!—2 Cor 5:17

This is all true to faith. But we must make it true in experience also; and here comes the struggle.

> For we know that our old self was crucified with him so that the body of sin might be rendered powerless, that we should no longer be slaves to sin. . . .
> In the same way, count yourselves dead to sin but alive to God in Christ Jesus.—Rom 6:6, 11

> You, however, did not come to know Christ that way. Surely you heard of him and were taught in him in accordance with the truth that is in Jesus. You were taught, with regard to your former way of life, to put off your old self, which is being corrupted by its deceitful desires; to be made new in the attitude of your minds; and to put on the new self, created to be like God in true righteousness and holiness.—Eph 4:20-24

We must "count" ourselves to be dead and alive again, by faith, on the authority of God's word, which declares that we are. We must "put off" our old self by faith, and "put on" the new self by faith also. And then we are to make this practical, by dying continually to the self-life, and by living only and always in the resurrection life. We must say with Paul, "I am crucified with Christ; nevertheless I live; and yet not I, but Christ lives in me"; and we must then act this out practically whenever the occasion arises. Our faith "counts" it, and the Lord enables us to make it real.

The faith that you can take a train and reach your destination in three days if only you buy your ticket, is a very different thing from the actual experience of the train ride itself. And in like manner, the faith, that in Christ you are already dead and risen, is a very different thing from the daily experience of "carrying in the body the death of Jesus, so that the life of Jesus may also be manifested in our bodies." The one is a *step* of faith, the other is a *life* of faith. The one may be momentary, the other must be lifelong.

> I tell you the truth, unless a kernel of wheat falls to the ground and dies, it remains only a single seed. But if it dies, it produces many seeds. The man who loves his life will lose it, while the man who hates his life in this world will keep it for eternal life. —Jn 12:24-25

There is no other way. The kernel of wheat must abide forever alone in itself, unless it die; and the soul must also. To "remain only a seed" in this sense means the awful solitude of the self-life, shut up to self, bounded and limited by self. What solitude could be more awful! But "if it dies it produces many seeds" and, therefore, much fruit. The resurrection life is abundant in fruit.

Joseph is a wonderful type of this resurrection life. It is a life which, from the first, dreams of victory and dominion over the things of time and sense; but which can only attain to this dominion through suffering. In a dream God revealed Joseph's future kingship to him.

> Joseph had a dream, and when he told it to his brothers, they hated him all the more. He said to them, "Listen to this dream I

had: We were binding sheaves of grain out in the field when suddenly my sheaf rose and stood upright, while your sheaves gathered around mine and bowed down to it."

His brothers said to him, "Do you intend to reign over us? Will you actually rule us?" And they hated him all the more because of his dream and what he had said.—Gn 37:5-8

His brethren hated him and called him a "dreamer." And souls that have had a sight of this resurrection life, and venture to speak of it, will often be hated also and called "mystics," and "dreamers"; and perhaps not even their brethren in the church will understand them.

If the world hates you, keep in mind that it hated me first. If you belonged to the world, it would love you as its own. As it is, you do not belong to the world, but I have chosen you out of the world. That is why the world hates you. Remember the words I spoke to you: "no servant is greater than his master."
—Jn 15:18-20 (Gn 37:19; Jn 17:14)

Joseph's exaltation and victory were sure to come, for God had declared it; but the road to them was by the way of trial, and suffering, and loss. It led through the pit, and through slavery, and through imprisonment in Egypt.

And they took him and threw him into the cistern. Now the cistern was empty; there was no water in it.
—Gn 37:24 (Gn 37:28; 39:20)

Through emptying to fullness, through abasement to exaltation, is always the way in this resurrection life. This is a necessity in the very nature of things.

If the butterfly life is to be born, the caterpillar life must die. The flesh-man must be put to death, if the spirit-man is to live. This is the explanation of the trial and suffering and loss that come to us all, as we advance in the divine life.

Whoever finds his life will lose it, and whoever loses his life for my sake will find it.—Mt 10:39 (Lk 9:24; Gal 15:24)

Through all its trials, the resurrection life reigns triumphant. It conquers by yielding, and reigns by serving. Joseph was a king, even in slavery or in prison.

> The Lord was with Joseph and he prospered, and he lived in the house of his Egyptian master. When his master saw that the Lord was with him and that the Lord gave him success in everything he did. . . .—Gn 39:2-3

> The Lord was with him; he showed him kindness and granted him favor in the eyes of the prison warden.—Gn 39:21

> Blessed are the poor in spirit, / for theirs is the kingdom of heaven. . . . / Blessed are the meek, / for they will inherit the earth. . . . / Blessed are those who are persecuted because of righteousness, / for theirs is the kingdom of heaven.   —Mt 5:3, 5, 10
> (Mt 5:11-12; Gn 39:4-6, 22-23; Mk 10:42-45)

Joseph's exaltation came at last, and the only road which could have brought him there, was through the very trials that had seemed as if they must crush him. God was in them all, and made out of each a chariot to carry him onward.

> Then Pharaoh said to Joseph, "Since God has made all this known to you, there is no one so discerning and wise as you. You shall be in charge of my palace, and all my people are to submit to your orders. Only with respect to the throne will I be greater than you."—Gn 41:39-40

> Then Joseph said to his brothers, "Come close to me." When they had done so, he said, "I am your brother Joseph, the one you sold into Egypt! And now, do not be distressed and do not be angry with yourselves for selling me here, because it was to save lives that God sent me ahead of you. . . . But God sent me ahead of you to preserve for you a remnant on earth and to save your lives by a great deliverance.
> So then, it was not you who sent me here, but God. He made me father to Pharaoh, lord of his entire household and ruler of all Egypt.—Gn 45:4-5, 7-8 (Gn 41:41-44)

"God sent me." Yes, through these very trials and apparent losses, God was leading his child onward to the fulfillment of his early dreams. And the soul now, that bows itself meekly to the yoke of trial and misunderstanding, and holds a steadfast faith through all, will find at last, as Joseph did, that these very trials have been God's chariots which have borne it in triumph to its longed-for exaltations. "if we suffer with Christ we shall also reign with him."

> But rejoice that you participate in the sufferings of Christ, so that you may be overjoyed when his glory is revealed. If you are insulted because of the name of Christ, you are blessed, for the Spirit of glory and of God rests on you.
>
> —1 Pt 4:13-14 (2 Cor 1:5-7)

The soul that suffers shall also reign. The things of time and sense shall be put under our feet, and we shall walk in the power of the resurrection life, as conquerors, through the very places where before we have been slaves and prisoners.

> Joseph named his firstborn Manasseh and said, "It is because God has made me forget all my trouble and all my father's household." The second son he named Ephraim and said, "it is because God has made me fruitful in the land of my suffering."—Gn 41:51-52

> Who shall separate us from the love of Christ? Shall trouble or hardship or persecution or famine or nakedness or danger or sword? As it is written:
> "For your sake we face death all day long; / we are considered as sheep to be slaughtered." / No, in all these things we are more than conquerors through him who loved us.
>
> —Rom 8:35-37

It is only the resurrection life that can be "more than conqueror" in a world like this. And who would not willingly and gladly lose his own self-life in order to find such an all-conquering life as this?

Consent then to die. Do not seek to improve or make more beautiful the caterpillar life, for no amount of beauty or improvement can turn the caterpillar into the butterfly. The transition can only come through death. Let the old self-life die then, that the new and risen life, that life which is hid with Christ in God, may have free scope to grow and develop. For thus and thus only shall you be able practically and triumphantly to be raised as Christ was raised, to "live a new life."

FOURTEEN

God's Workmanship

Foundation Text— *For we are God's workmanship, created in Christ Jesus to do good works, which God prepared in advance for us to do.* —Eph 2:10

To be "God's workmanship" means that God is our Maker, and that he will make us into the thing that will please him, if we do not take ourselves out of his forming hands.

> Know that the Lord is God. / It is he who made us, and we are his; / we are his people, the sheep of his pasture.
> —Ps 100:3 (Ps 119:73; 139:14-16)

It takes us a great while to learn that God is really our Maker, and not we ourselves; and a large part of the perplexities of our spiritual experience arise from this ignorance. We are continually taking ourselves out of the hands of our Divine Maker by our efforts to make, or remake, or unmake ourselves. The Potter desires to fashion us into a beautiful vessel for his honor, but we will not hold still and let him work. We interfere with his processes, either by resisting him, or by trying to help him, and so the vessel is "marred in his hands."

> So I went down to the potter's house, and I saw him working at the wheel. But the pot he was shaping from the clay was marred in

his hands; so the potter formed it into another pot, shaping it as seemed best to him.

Then the word of the Lord came to me; "O house of Israel, can I not do with you as this potter does?" declares the Lord. "Like clay in the hand of the potter, so are you in my hand, O house of Israel. —Jer 18:3-6

If we realize that we are God's workmanship and not our own, we will lie still in his hands, and will abandon ourselves to his working without a care.

Yet, O Lord, you are our Father. / We are the clay, you are the potter; / we are all the work of your hand. —Is 64:8

God's workmanship, where he has his own way unhindered, must be like himself, perfect. And therefore he can command us in our weakness to be perfect because he is our Maker, and he knows that his purpose is to make us perfect. We are to be made into something that will be to his glory.

He is the Rock, his works are perfect, / and all his ways are just. / A faithful God who does no wrong, / upright and just is he.
—Dt 32:4

Be perfect, therefore, as your heavenly Father is perfect.
—Mt 5:48 (Is 43:21; 1 Pt 2:9)

The glory of a man is shown forth in his work, and the glory of God must shine forth in the "works of his hands." A good workman cannot produce poor workmanship. Therefore, if we will only abandon ourselves to God's working, he will without fail prepare good works for us to do.

Praise be to the God and Father of our Lord Jesus Christ, who has blessed us in the heavenly realms with every spiritual blessing in Christ. For he chose us in him before the creation of the world to be holy and blameless in his sight. In love he predestined us to be adopted as his sons through Jesus Christ, in accordance with his pleasure and will—to the praise of his glorious grace, which he has freely given us in the One he loves. . . . in order that we, who were the first to hope in Christ, might be for the praise of his glory.—Eph 1:3-6, 12

This was his purpose in our creation at first, for we were to be made in his "own image."

Then God said, "Let us make man in our image, in our likeness, and let them rule over the fish of the sea and the birds of the air, over the livestock, over all the earth, and over all the creatures that move along the ground.
So God created man in his own image, in the image of God he created him; male and female he created them.—Gn 1:26-27

Of course this did not mean a likeness of person or body, but a likeness of character and nature; that is, we are "to be perfect as he is perfect," i.e., in the same sort of perfection, not as to degree of course, but as to quality. We cannot see God to know what we are to be like; but we see him incarnated in Christ, who is declared to be the "express image" of God; and thus we can look upon and consider the image to which we are to be conformed.

For those God foreknew he also predestined to be conformed to the likeness of his Son, that he might be the firstborn among many brothers.—Rom 8:29

Since Christ was the "express image" of God, and we are to be conformed to the image of Christ, we can see how the Divine purpose in our creation is to be brought about.

Do not lie to each other, since you have taken off your old self with its practices and have put on the new self, which is being renewed in knowledge in the image of its Creator.—Col 3:9-10

To be made new in the attitude of your minds; and to put on the new self, created to be like God in true righteousness and holiness.—Eph 4:23-24

To make us then in his "own image," is therefore the object of God's workmanship, and nothing short of this will accomplish his divine purpose in our creation.

We can never understand a complicated machine until we know what was the purpose of the maker in regard to it. How did he mean it to work; what was it intended to accomplish; how has he arranged for it to run? When we walk through an exhibition of machinery we ask continually, as we stop to look at one machine after another, "What is this for?" "What is that for?" We are sure, when we see a machine, that the maker intended it to accomplish some special end; and we cannot imagine any man being so stupid as to make a machine that is not meant to accomplish anything.

Our Divine Maker therefore has made us for something. And it is essential for us to find out what this is before we can expect to accomplish it. What then are we made to be, and what are we to do?

> Everyone who is called by my name, / whom I created for my glory, / whom I formed and made.—Is 43:7

We are made then to bring glory to our Maker by perfectly fulfilling his purposes in our creation.

A machine that fails to fulfill the purposes of its maker, does not bring honor, but dishonor, upon him. And we who fail in fulfilling the purposes of our Creator, are bringing dishonor upon him. What then is this purpose?

> You made him a little lower than the heavenly beings / and crowned him with glory and honor. / You made him ruler over the works of your hands; / you put everything under his feet.
> —Ps 8:5-6

He has made us rulers. We are to be kings. We are to sit on the throne with Christ, and reign with him over the things of time and sense. We are to conquer the world, instead of being conquered by it. We are to know what it is to be made "always to triumph" through Christ. If we fail in this victory; if, instead of having dominion over sin, sin has "dominion" over us, if the world and the things of it master us and bring us into bondage we are not fulfilling the purposes of our Creator, and are therefore bringing disgrace upon his name.

And to make all men see what is the plan of the mystery hidden for ages in God who created all things; that through the church the manifold wisdom of God might now be made known to the principalities and powers in the heavenly places. This was according to the eternal purpose which he has realized in Christ Jesus our Lord.—Eph 3:9-11 RSV

If the "manifold wisdom of God" is to be shown forth in us and by us to the principalities and powers in heavenly places, we must try to discover how it can be accomplished. We ask of a complicated machine, how does it operate? And we mean, how do its different parts move in reference to one another, and what is the power that keeps them in motion. If a machine operates the way its maker meant it to, it will move easily and without friction. And we can only have easy and frictionless lives, if our inward machinery moves according to the divine plan. My hand was made to shut inward on my palm, and it shuts that way easily and without friction. But if I try to shut it outward over on its back, I cannot do it without breaking something. My heart was made to love and serve its Creator, and when I do this, all my inward machinery moves without friction or jar. But if I love and serve the creature more than the Creator, all goes wrong, and something is sure to break.

A great deal of the friction and failure in our spiritual lives arise from this fact, that we do not operate as God meant us to.

Therefore, my dear friends, as you have always obeyed—not only in my presence, but now much more in my absence—continue to work out your salvation with fear and trembling, for it is God who works in you to will and to act according to his good purpose.—Phil 2:12-13

Paul does not say work *for* your salvation, but work *out* the salvation which God is working *in* you. We try to work things according to our own wills, not according to his will, and the result is as if an ignorant man should undertake to work a complicated machine after his own notions, instead of following the directions of its maker.

> To this end I labor, struggling with all his energy, which so powerfully works in me.—Col 1:29

Our "struggling" must be "with all his energy" or it will amount to nothing.

> I pray also that the eyes of your heart may be enlightened in order that you may know the hope to which he has called you, the riches of his glorious inheritance in the saints, and his incomparably great power for us who believe.—Eph 1:18-19 (Col 1:10-11)

Every machine of man's making is intended to operate by some definite sort of power, by manpower, by water power, or by some other method. In every case the machine is made for its own power, and will not operate for any other.

We are made to go by Holy Spirit power, and we cannot go right without it.

> But you will receive power when the Holy Spirit comes on you; and you will be my witnesses in Jerusalem, and in all Judea and Samaria, and to the ends of the earth.—Acts 1:8

If we try to work ourselves by our own power we shall utterly fail, for we have no natural powers that can control spiritual forces. Only the powers that belong to the spiritual nature can have dominion over these.

> Unless the Lord builds the house, / its builders labor in vain. / Unless the Lord watches over the city, / the watchmen stand guard in vain. / In vain you rise early / and stay up late, / toiling for food to eat— / for he grants sleep to those he loves.
> —Ps 127:1-2

> Remain in me, and I will remain in you. No branch can bear fruit by itself; it must remain in the vine. Neither can you bear fruit unless you remain in me.
> I am the vine; you are the branches. If a man remains in me and I

in him, he will bear much fruit; apart from me you can do nothing. If anyone does not remain in me, he is like a branch that is thrown away and withers; such branches are picked up, thrown into the fire and burned. —Jn 15:4-6

In order then to be what we were intended by our Maker to be, and to work as we were intended by him to work, we must recognize the fact that we are his workmanship, and must abandon ourselves to his working.

May the God of peace, who through the blood of the eternal covenant brought back from the dead our Lord Jesus, that great Shepherd of the sheep, equip you with everything good for doing his will, and may he work in us what is pleasing to him, through Jesus Christ, to whom be glory for ever and ever. Amen. —Heb 13:20-21 (Acts 17:24-26; 2 Cor 5:5; Acts 19:11)

There is nothing more plainly told us in the Bible than just this fact, that we are God's workmanship, and that whatever true or acceptable work we do must be by his "working in us what is pleasing to him." And yet plainly as this is taught, there is scarcely anything we practically believe less.

We use the words, "The Lord my Maker," over and over, but they convey no clear idea to our minds; and we go on trying to make ourselves, working at our own interior life, and exhausting ourselves in efforts to transform our characters into a likeness to Christ. We try to "create" ourselves to good works, and are in despair at our continual failures.

For in my inner being I delight in God's law; but I see another law at work in the members of my body, waging war against the law of my mind and making me a prisoner of the law of sin at work within my members. What a wretched man I am! Who will rescue me from this body of death? —Rom 7:22-24

When however we recognize the fact that God is really our Maker, not only in the outward creation but in the inward as well; and further when we see that he is also our re-Creator in redemption, we shall be forced to realize that he is therefore the only one who can understand how to work us, and who can remake us when we mar his work. If our watches are out of order, we do not meddle with them ourselves, but we take them to a man who makes watches, and who therefore knows how to remake them. And similarly must we do in our own case. If we are out of order we must take ourselves to the One who made us, and leave ourselves in his hands to be remade according to his divine plan.

> Therefore, I urge you, brothers, in view of God's mercy, to offer your bodies as living sacrifices, holy and pleasing to God—which is your spiritual worship. Do not conform any longer to the pattern of this world, but be transformed by the renewing of your mind. Then you will be able to test and approve what God's will is—his good, pleasing and perfect will.—Rom 12:1-2

What we need is to be "transformed," and none but the Lord can do this. Our only hope therefore is in letting him have his own way with us, by abandoning ourselves utterly to him to be put in order, as a watch is abandoned to the watchmaker. We do not understand the watchmaker's processes with our watches, and it may well be that we shall not understand the Lord's processes with ourselves.

> As you do not know the path of the wind, / or how the body is formed in a mother's womb, / so you cannot understand the work of God, / the Maker of all things.—Eccl 11:5

> Woe to him who quarrels with his Maker, / to him who is but a potsherd among the potsherds on the ground. / Does the clay say to the potter, / "What are you making?" / Does your work say, / "He has no hands?" / Woe to him who says to his father, / "What have you begotten?" / or to his mother, / "What have you brought to birth?"—Is 45:9-10 (Is 45:11-12; Rom 11:33-34, 36)

Since we will all acknowledge that his ways are truly beyond understanding we must be content to leave the management of ourselves in his hands, and must believe that his dealings with us are the very best that could be, even though they may seem to us very mysterious or painful.

And you have forgotten that word of encouragement that addresses you as sons:

> "My son, do not make light of the Lord's discipline, / and do not lose heart when he rebukes you, / because the Lord disciplines those he loves, / and he punishes everyone he accepts as a son." Endure hardship as discipline; God is treating you as sons. For what son is not disciplined by his father?—Heb 12:5-7 (Heb 12:8-11)

The trial which is so hard to bear is one of God's blessed disciplinary actions, without which your soul would never have known its fullest glory.

> But thou art making me; I thank thee, Sire.
> What thou hast done and doest, thou knowest well;
> And I will help thee: gently in thy fire
> I will lie burning; on thy potter's wheel
> I will whirl patient, though my brain should reel;
> Thy grace shall be enough my grief to quell,
> And growing beauty shine through suffering dire.
> Too eager I must not be to understand.
> How should the work the Master goes about
> Fit the vague sketch my compasses have planned?
>
> I am his house, for him to go in and out;
> He builds me now, and if I cannot see
> At any time what he is doing with me
> 'Tis that he makes the house for me too grand.

The wondrous end of God's making is, that we are to bear his own image, and who can marvel if the process by which this is to be accomplished may be sometimes hard and painful.

Therefore we do not lose heart. Though outwardly we are wasting away, yet inwardly we are being renewed day by day. For our light and momentary troubles are achieving for us an eternal glory that far outweighs them all.—2 Cor 4:16-17

And we, who with unveiled faces all reflect the Lord's glory, are being transformed into his likeness with every-increasing glory, which comes from the Lord, who is the Spirit.—2 Cor 3:18

We have only to watch the making processes which all beautiful works of art require to bring them to perfection, in order to comprehend the reason of our trials.

'Tis that I am not good, that is enough,
I pry no farther; that is not the way.
Here, oh my Potter, is thy making stuff!
Set thy wheel going; let it whirl and play.
The chips in me, the stones, the straw, the sand,
Cast them out with fine separating hand,
And make a vessel of thy yielding clay.

There is infinite comfort and rest of soul in the fact that we are God's workmanship and not our own; for it gives us an unanswerable claim upon him.

The Lord will fulfill his purpose for me; / your love, O Lord, endures forever— / do not abandon the works of your hands.
—Ps 138:8 (Job 10:8-12)

The responsibility of creatorship is absolute. It is recognized all the world over in the responsibilities of parents for their children whom they have brought into existence. He who brings a being into existence is bound, we instinctively feel, to care for that being in the very best way possible.

"Why then did you bring me out of the womb? / I wish I had died before any eye saw me. / If only I had never come into being, / or had been carried straight from the womb to the grave!"
—Job 10:18-19

Our God himself recognizes this responsibility of creatorship.

Remember these things, O Jacob, / for you are my servant, O
Israel. / I have made you, you are my servant; / O Israel, I will not
forget you.—Is 44:21

So then, those who suffer according to God's will should commit
themselves to their faithful Creator and continue to do good.
—1 Pt 4:19 (Is 44:2-3)

He is called our "faithful Creator" and because he is faithful
we are urged to commit the keeping of our souls to him, for he
himself has declared "I have made you and I will bear you; I
will sustain you and I will receive you. (Is 46:4)
We used to be frightened sometimes at the words "Remember your Creator," as though they were the demand of
something awful and alarming. But now we see that we could
not "remember" a more blessed, or lovely, or restful fact. For
our Creator is also our Saviour.

"You are my witnesses," declares the Lord, / "and my servant
whom I have chosen, / so that you may know and believe me / and
understand that I am he. / Before me no god was formed, / nor
will there be one after me. / I, even I, am the Lord, / and apart
from me there is no savior. / I have revealed and saved and
proclaimed— / I, and not some foreign god among you. / You
are my witnesses," declares the Lord, "that I am God. / Yes, and
from ancient days I am he. / No one can deliver out of my hand. /
When I act, who can reverse it?"—Is 43:10-13 (Is 45:17-22)

God made, and he will remake. We were his workmanship in
creation, and we are his workmanship in redemption. And he
takes pleasure in his own work.

For the Lord takes pleasure in his people; / he adorns the humble
with victory.—Ps 149:4 RSV (Ps 147:11; Rv 4:11)

It is a universal instinct to take pleasure in anything we
create. How we look at it, and turn it round to view it on every

side, and walk off to see it at a distance, and delight to show it to those who will appreciate it and share our pleasure.

God saw all that he had made, and it was very good.—Gn 1:31

When we look on man as he is now, and when we hear the groans and cries of creation, we wonder that God could call his work "very good." But in redemption we behold the consummation of this work which in creation was only begun, and see God's ultimate purpose for man carried out, and the excellence of his work manifested.

To illustrate, we have the declaration that man is "made a ruler," but in Hebrews we are told that this is not yet seen: "Yet at present we do not see everything subject to him. But we see Jesus."

In putting everything under him, God left nothing that is not subject to him. Yet at present we do not see everything subject to him. But we see Jesus, who was made a little lower than the angels, now crowned with glory and honor because he suffered death, so that by the grace of God he might taste death for everyone.

In bringing many sons to glory, it was fitting that God, for whom and through whom everything exists, should make the author of their salvation perfect through suffering. Both the one who makes men holy and those who are made holy are of the same family. So Jesus is not ashamed to call them brothers.

—Heb 2:8-11

Jesus therefore is the Head of the new redeemed spiritual race who are to fulfill God's purposes in creation, just as Adam was the head of the present imperfect earthly race. And as we have borne the image of the one, so are we to bear finally the image of the other.

So it is written: "The first man Adam became a living being"; the last Adam, a life-giving spirit. The spiritual did not come first, but the natural, and after that the spiritual. The first man was of the dust of the earth, the second man from heaven. As was the earthly man, so are those who are of the earth; and as is the man from heaven, so also are those who are of heaven. And just as we have borne the likeness of the earthly man, so shall we bear the likeness of the man from heaven.—1 Cor 15:45-49

This, then, as we have seen, is the ultimate purpose of God's workmanship, to conform us to the image of his Son, "created in Christ Jesus to do good works." And he alone is able to accomplish such a mighty transformation. Let us then take our own hands off of ourselves, and put ourselves unreservedly into the hands of the Lord, believing that, although *we* are not able, *he* is able: and that nothing is too hard for his almighty power.

And God is able to make all grace abound to you, so that in all things at all times, having all that you need, you will abound in every good work.—2 Cor 9:8 (Eph 3:20-21)

Nothing can give more utter rest of soul than this. If we are "God's workmanship," and if he is making us, we cannot find any room for fear or anxiety. No matter how bad we may feel ourselves to be, no matter how grievously out of order our inward machinery may seem, if God has us in his workshop and if he is at work on us, how can we have a care as to the result?

Moreover if we are God's workmanship we may be very sure of his abiding presence with us; for a man who is making anything must necessarily be close to it all the time he is at work on it. "What can there be so close as making and made?" Therefore, while God's blessed processes are going on, we cannot have a doubt or a question about his continual presence with us.

God's part then is to work, and our part is to abandon ourselves utterly to his working, and to see to it that we do not hinder him by disobedience or doubt. He has undertaken to "create us in Christ Jesus to do good works," and we must yield ourselves up submissively to his blessed making processes, and must be content with the way of his working. We must yield, and trust, and obey without wavering, come what may; and we must never be discouraged because we do not see ourselves perfect all at once. "The Maker hath not done" yet, but he will assuredly perfect that which concerns us at last.

'Tis, shall thy will be done for me? or mine,
And I be made a thing not after thine,
My own, and full of paltriest pretense?
Shall I be born of God, or of mere man?
Be made like Christ, or on some other plan?
What though thy work in me transcends my sense,
Too fine, too high, for me to understand,
I trust entirely. On, Lord, with thy labor grand!
I have not knowledge, wisdom, insight, thought,
Nor understanding, fit to justify
Thee in thy work, O Perfect. Thou hast brought
me up to this; and lo! what thou hast wrought
I cannot call it good. But I can cry
"O enemy, the Maker hath not done;
One day thou shalt behold, and from the sight will run.'

FIFTEEN

The Presence of God

"Thus doth thy hospitable greatness lie
Outside us like a boundless sea;
We cannot lose ourselves where all is home,
Nor drift away from thee."

Foundation Text— *Where can I go from your Spirit? /*
Where can I flee from your presence / If I go up to the heavens,
you are there; / if I make my bed in the depths, you are there. /
If I rise on the wings of the dawn, / if I settle on the far side of
the sea, / even there your hand will guide me, / your right
hand will hold me fast. —Ps 139:7-10

The all-pervading presence of God with us is the one
absolutely certain and unchangeable thing amid all that is so
doubtful and changeable in this world of ours. And yet very
few people realize this. Even Christians will cry out for the
Lord to "come" to them, as though he had gone off on a
journey or were in the remote realms of space. "How can I get
into his presence?" they ask with eager longing; when all the
while they are already in his presence, and cannot by any
possibility get out of it, not even if they "make their bed in
hell," or if they live in the furthest part of the earth. "Even
there," wherever it may be, shall his hand hold and lead them.

> Then the man and his wife heard the sound of the Lord God as he was walking in the garden in the cool of the day, and they hid from the Lord God among the trees of the garden.—Gn 3:8

At this early period of human history we find that the Lord was present with the man and woman whom he had made. And from this time onward all through the ages, he is seen to be in continual daily and familiar intercourse with his people.

In Exodus he commanded them to make a sanctuary.

> Then have them make a sanctuary for me, and I will dwell among them—Ex 25:8 (Ex 29:45-46)

We are told that he walked with them in the wilderness.

> Because the Lord your God walks in the midst of your camp, to save you and to give up your enemies before you, therefore your camp must be holy, that he may not see anything indecent among you, and turn away from you.—Dt 23:14 RSV (2 Sm 7:4-6)

When they took up their abode in the promised land, he commanded them to build a house for his name.

> My father David had it in his heart to build a temple for the Name of the Lord, the God of Israel. But the Lord said to my father David, "Because it was in your heart to build a temple for my Name, you did well to have this in your heart. Nevertheless, you are not the one to build the temple, but your son, who is your own flesh and blood—he is the one who will build the temple for my Name. . . ."
> But will God really dwell on earth with men? The heavens cannot contain you. How much less this temple I have built!
> —2 Chr 6:7-9, 18

When this house was finished, he took up his abode in it, that he might dwell in the midst of his people continually, as their ever-present neighbor and friend.

> When the priests withdrew from the Holy Place, the cloud filled the temple of the Lord. And the priests could not perform their service because of the cloud, for the glory of the Lord filled his temple.

Then Solomon said, "The Lord has said that he would dwell in a dark cloud; I have indeed built a magnificent temple for you, a place for you to dwell forever.—1 Kgs 8:10-13

I have chosen and consecrated this temple so that my Name may be there forever. My eyes and my heart will always be there.
—2 Chr 7:16

When Solomon finished praying, fire came down from heaven and consumed the burnt offering and the sacrifices, and the glory of the Lord filled the temple. The priests could not enter the temple of the Lord because the glory of the Lord filled it.
—2 Chr 7:1-2 (2 Chr 7:12-15)

Through all the back-sliding of the children of Israel, and through all their rebellions, he remained with them, and never ceased urging them to trust fully in him, and to abandon the whole management of their lives to his care.

In all their distress he too was distressed, / and the angel of his presence saved them. / In his love and mercy he redeemed them; / he lifted them up and carried them / all the days of old.
—Is 63:9 (1 Chr 17:8)

And finally, in Christ, God came down in bodily form, and walked and lived among us, a man like us, taking upon himself our nature and sharing our common lot. His very name, "God with us," tells us the whole wonderful story, that God, our Creator is not a distant God dwelling in unapproachable mystery, but is near at hand to every one of us, closer to us even than we are to ourselves, for "in him we live and move and have our being."

God did this so that men would seek him and perhaps reach out for him and find him, though he is not far from each one of us. "For in him we live and move and have our being." As some of your own poets have said, "We are his offspring."—Acts 17:27-28

In Christ, God linked himself to humanity openly and forever, and thus revealed to us the fact of his abiding presence with humanity always and everywhere; so that we must never think of a single human being as apart from him.

The Word became flesh and lived for a while among us. We have seen his glory, the glory of the one and only Son, who came from the Father, full of grace and truth.—Jn 1:14

Since the children have flesh and blood, he too shared in their humanity so that by his death he might destroy him who holds the power of death—that is, the devil—and free those who all their lives were held in slavery by their fear of death. For surely it is not angels he helps, but Abraham's descendants. For this reason he had to be made like his brothers in every way, in order that he might become a merciful and faithful high priest in service to God, and that he might make atonement for the sins of the people.—Heb 2:14-17 (Phil 2:5-8; 1 Tm 3:16)

This then is a settled fact that cannot be questioned, that God *is* with us always, nearer to us than we are to ourselves, no matter whether we are conscious of his presence or not.

Speak to him, thou, for he hears,
and spirit with spirit may meet;
Closer is he than breathing,
and nearer than hands and feet.

For you created my inmost being; / you knit me together in my mother's womb.—Ps 139:13

Human language could not express a greater nearness than this; and to doubt it, is to doubt the whole revelation of the Bible.

Lord, you have been our dwelling place / throughout all generations.—Ps 90:1

Since God has been our dwelling place throughout all generations, we surely must not begin to question or doubt it now. We will therefore consider next what this fact is to mean practically in our daily lives.

It means I am sure far more of inward rest and peace than most people believe to be possible in this world of care and trouble.

We all know the rest that comes, even in the midst of trouble, from the presence of a tried and trusted friend. We sometimes say of such a friend, "She is a tower of strength to me"; and we express in these words the same thought humanly applied, which contains a divine application when we say of the Lord that he is our "strong tower" to whom we may continually resort.

> I love you, O Lord my strength. / The Lord is my rock, my fortress and my deliverer; / my God is my rock, in whom I take refuge. / He is my shield and the horn of my salvation, my stronghold.—Ps 18:1-2

> From the ends of the earth I call to you, / I call as my heart grows faint; / lead me to the rock that is higher than I. / For you have been my refuge, / a strong tower against the foe. / I long to dwell in your tent forever / and take refuge in the shelter of your wings.—Ps 61:2-4

God's abiding presence with us means the solution of every difficulty of our lives. The mother's presence with the child solves all the child's difficulties; just her simple presence, without need of any special promises or assurances. "Oh, there is my mother!" the little troubled child will exclaim, and at the sight of her coming, all the childish burdens will drop off and vanish.

> The Lord replied, "My Presence will go with you, and I will give you rest."—Ex 33:14

How often in our childhood, when we have been afraid to go somewhere or to do something, have our mothers comforted us, saying, "I will be with you," and how often has God stilled all the fears of his people by the same simple announcement, "Certainly, I will be with you."

> But Moses said to God, "Who am I, that I should go to Pharaoh and bring the Israelites out of Egypt?"
> And God said, "I will be with you. And this will be the sign to

you that it is I who have sent you: When you have brought the people out of Egypt, you will worship God on this mountain."
—Ex 3:11-12

Then Jesus came to them and said, "All authority in heaven and on earth has been given to me. Therefore go and make disciples of all nations, baptizing them in the name of the Father and of the Son and of the Holy Spirit, and teaching them to obey everything I have commanded you. And surely I will be with you always, to the very end of the age.'—Mt 28:18-20 (Jos 1:5, 9)

We cannot doubt that all these reiterated assurances of his presence with his people, under all their varying circumstances and conditions, *must* be meant to assure us, that, because he is thus with us, we may be also sure that all he has of wisdom or of power are at our disposal, and are engaged on our behalf. No good mother *could* be present with her child, and fail to use all her resources in that child's behalf; her mother-heart would make it impossible. And the heart of God towards us makes it far more impossible for him to be present with us and fail to help us in every need.

"Ah, Sovereign Lord," I said, "I do not know how to speak; I am only a child."
But the Lord said to me, "Do not say, 'I am only a child.' You must go to everyone I send you to and say whatever I command you. Do not be afraid of them, for I am with you and will rescue you," declares the Lord.—Jer 1:6-8

"I am with you and will rescue you; this is the express object of my being with you, this is just what I am for; therefore be not afraid." Two little girls were once talking together when one began to tell the other of her fright in the dark. "Oh," replied the other eagerly, "I do not see how you *can* be afraid when God is always taking care of us." "But," said the first, "I don't believe God does take care of such little girls as us." "Why, Mollie," exclaimed her little friend in surprise, "don't you know that that is just what God is for!"

But I will rescue you on that day, declares the Lord; you will not be handed over to those you fear. I will save you; you will not fall by the sword but will escape with your life, because you trust in me, declares the Lord.—Jer 39:17-18

It is a sad fact that in spite of these reiterated assertions of our Lord's, only a few of his people really believe in his abiding presence. They will all perhaps *say* they do, but when it comes down to their real belief, behind their words, it is manifest that it is nothing more than a pious sentiment, and has no practical reality whatever to their souls. Else, why the fear and trouble of heart that render so many Christian lives miserable? To the soul that believes in his presence as a *literal fact*, there can never be anything but joyous triumph or peaceful calm. That soul *has God*, and it knows that God is sufficient. His simple presence is a certain assurance of all possible care and help.

"Shout and be glad, O Daughter of Zion. For I am coming, and I will live among you," declares the Lord.—Zc 2:10

His presence is enough for our joy, let what else come or go. We have all of us known loved ones in our lives, whose mere presence brought with it always utter content. A prison would have been a palace with that one's presence in it; and without that one, nothing had any joy.

Though the fig tree does not bud / and there are no grapes on the vines, / though the olive crop fails / and the fields produce no food, / though there are no sheep in the pen / and no cattle in the stalls, / Yet I will rejoice in the Lord, / I will be joyful in God my Savior. / The Sovereign Lord is my strength; / he makes my feet like the feet of a deer, / he enables me to go on the heights.
—Hb 3:17-19

Madame Guyon expresses it as follows;

All scenes alike engaging prove
To souls impressed with sacred love;

Where'er they dwell, they dwell in thee,
In Heaven, in earth, or on the sea.
To me remains nor place, nor time,
My country is in every clime;
I can be calm and free from care,
On any shore, since God is there.
While place we seek or place we shun
The soul finds happiness in none;
But with my God to guide the way
'Tis equal joy to go or stay.
Could I be cast where thou wert not,
That were indeed a dreadful lot;
But regions none remote I call,
Secure of finding God in all.

"Can anyone hide in secret places / so that I cannot see him?" declares the Lord. / "Do not I fill heaven and earth?" declares the Lord.—Jer 23:24

He who "fills heaven and earth" must surely be in the places he fills; even though we may not see him or feel him there.

If I say, "Surely the darkness will hide me / and the light become night around me," / even the darkness will not be dark to you; / the night will shine like the day, / for darkness is as light to you.—Ps 139:11-12

"Even the darkness will not be dark to you." We all know this must be a fact, in the very nature of things; and yet when the soul finds itself in spiritual darkness, it seems impossible to believe that it can be true. The fever of delirium may hide the mother from the child, and her heart may be wrung by its piteous cries for her coming, but the child's blindness does not drive away the mother nor make her ears deaf to its cries. And just so the delirium of our doubts or despair, or even of our sins, while it hides him from us, so that we call out in anguish for his presence, can never hide us from him, for the "darkness is as light" to him.

If our faith will but grasp this fact as a reality, our "seasons of darkness" will not trouble us, for we shall be sure all the while, although we cannot see him nor feel him, that he is still there close at hand for our need, an "ever present" help in all our trouble.

God is our refuge and strength, / an ever present help in trouble. / Therefore we will not fear, though the earth give way / and the mountains fall into the heart of the sea, / though its waters roar and foam / and the mountains quake with their surging.
—Ps 46:1-3

Yet I am always with you; / you hold me by my right hand. / You guide me with your counsel, / and afterward you will take me into glory. / Whom have I in heaven but you? / And being with you, I desire nothing on earth. / My flesh and my heart may fail, / but God is the strength of my heart / and my portion forever.
—Ps 73:23-26

"Flesh and heart may fail," but the ever-present God still holds us by our right hand, even though we may not realize it, and is our all sufficient portion for ever.

Thou hast ascended on high, / thou hast led captivity captive: / thou hast received gifts for men; / yea, for the rebellious also, / that the Lord God might dwell among them. / Blessed be the Lord, / who daily loadeth us with benefits, / even the God of our salvation.—Ps 68:18-19 KJV (Ps 61:2-4)

Neither can any backsliding take us out of his presence. No matter how far away our souls may seem to wander, though it should be to the "far side of the sea," yet "even there" we shall always find him with us, prepared to "Load us with benefits" the moment we are ready to receive them.

Give thanks to the Lord, for he is good; / his love endures forever. Let the redeemed of the Lord say this— / those he redeemed from the hand of the foe, / those he gathered from the lands, / from east and west, from north and south. / Some wandered in desert wastelands, / finding no way to a city where they could settle. / The were hungry and thirsty, / and their lives ebbed away.

Then they cried out to the Lord in their trouble, / and he delivered them from their distress. / He led them by a straight way/ to a city where they could settle. / Let them give thanks to the Lord for his unfailing love / and his wonderful deeds for men.—Ps 107:1-8

I am sure we all *would* praise him instinctively and without effort for his wonderful works, if we would only believe in their reality. And I want us therefore to see him as this ever-present God, always close at hand to hear and to help, let us have wandered where we may.

But some may ask whether there is not such a thing as "coming into" his presence and "leaving" it, being nearer or further off from him. To this I answer that these are only figures of speech which express spiritual states on our part, and not any divine facts on his part. I may be seated close to a person and yet be in spirit separated from that person thousands of miles. And when we speak of nearness or distance as regards God, it is only according to our spirits, not according to the facts. He is always near us, but we are not always near him. In fact he is never far enough off even to be spoken of as near. He "created us in our inmost being," and if we only knew the facts of the case, it would be as impossible for us to think of ourselves apart from him, as to think of ourselves apart from ourselves.

I feel sure our modes of speech in regard to this subject have led us into great darkness. We pray, "O Lord, come to us" When we ought to pray, "O Lord, make us come!" The "coming" is altogether in our spirits, not in his presence.

As the mountains are round about Jerusalem, / so the Lord is round about his people, / from this time forth and for evermore.
—Ps 125:2

How *are* the mountains round about Jerusalem? Are they there today, and gone to-morrow? Are they there in sunshine, but do they forsake Jerusalem when it storms? Are they there when all eyes see them, but gone when night makes them invisible?

You exclaim, "What foolish questions!" But if the "as" and "so" in this verse are true, and if the Lord really is round about his people *as* the mountains are round about Jerusalem, the things many Christians think and say are far more foolish. Did none of you ever think in time of trouble and darkness that the Lord had forsaken you?

Suppose the dwellers in Jerusalem had acted toward their mountains as some of you act toward your God, what would you have thought of them? Suppose they had said on sunshiny days, "Now we believe the mountains surround us, because we can see them." And then on stormy days had said, "Alas! there are no mountains around us, for we cannot see them any longer!

It is an unchangeable fact that the mountains *are* round about Jerusalem, whether any one sees them or not; and it is equally an unchangeable fact that God *is* always round about us "from this time forth and for evermore," whether we see and feel him or not.

> The angel of the Lord encamps around those who fear him, / and he delivers them.—Ps 34:7

> God is within her, she will not fall; / God will help her at break of day.—Ps 46:5

Since, therefore, God encamps round about us, and is in our midst, since in short, he is our continual environment, we must not *allow* ourselves to be moved, for it would bring dishonor on his power or willingness to save. Nothing can harm the child in the mother's presence, unless the mother is first disabled. And since our God cannot be disabled, nothing can hurt or destroy us in his presence. In fact nothing can withstand the mighty, all-conquering power of his presence. Mountains and oceans and rocks and deserts in the spiritual realms of life melt and vanish when he appears.

The mountains melt like wax before the Lord, / before the Lord of all the earth. / The earth shook, / the heavens poured down rain, / before God, the One of Sinai, / before God, the God of Israel.—Ps 68:8 (Ps 114:7-8)

Neither men nor devils can harm the soul that abides in his presence.

How great is your goodness, / which you have stored up for those who fear you, / which you bestow in the sight of men / on those who take refuge in you. / In the shelter of your presence you hide them / from the intrigues of men; / in your dwelling you keep them safe / from the strife of tongues.
                                                    —Ps 31:19-20 (Heb 13:5-6)

The "secret of his presence" is a secret *open* to all, but not *opened* to every one. Nature was an open secret before all men in Newton's day, but it was *opened* to Newton only. The soul that has discovered this secret of God's presence has entered into his dwelling where nothing can ever disturb its rest, for nothing disturbing can find the "hidden" soul.

Thou has beset me behind and before, / and laid thine hand upon me—Ps 139:5 KJV

Have you ever thought of what it means to be "beset" by God? We understand what it is to be so "beset" sometimes by unwelcome and disagreeable people as not to be able to get rid of them, rebuff them as we may. If God "besets" us then, it must mean that he is so close to us in love and care, that no indifference nor even rebuffs on our part can force him to leave us.

Moreover he besets us "behind," that is he goes after us to set straight the things we have made crooked, and to undo the mistakes and failures that lie behind us. Mothers do this for their children all their lives beginning with picking up the scattered toys in the nursery, and going "behind" them as they grow older to undo and atone for all their mistakes. When a troubled, frightened child tells its mother of its wrong doing, and asks her sympathy and help, how ready is the mother's ear to listen and her heart to devise ways of help. Suppose the trouble *has* been all the child's fault, nonetheless is the mother willing and eager to help it. And nonetheless God is willing and eager to help us, even though our troubles come from our own fault.

If, therefore, we have in our past any mistake or sin which is a present source of distress to us, let us commit it with confidence to the God who is "behind" us, sure that he will make all things, even these very failures, work together for good for ourselves and others, if we will but trust him.

> And we know that in all things God works for the good of those who love him, who have been called according to his purpose.
> —Rom 8:28 (Jl 2:25-27)

Not only peace however, but holiness also, will be the result of God's recognized presence.

> Don't you know that you yourselves are God's temple and that God's Spirit lives in you? If anyone destroys God's temple, God will destroy him; for God's temple is sacred, and you are that temple.—1 Cor 3:16-17 (2 Cor 6:16; Ps 93:5)

The presence of God will drive out sin, as sunshine drives out darkness, if the heart will but open itself to his shining.

> This is the message we have heard form him and declare to you: God is light; in him there is no darkness at all. If we claim to have fellowship with him yet walk in the darkness, we lie and do not live by the truth. But if we walk in the light, as he is in the light, we have fellowship with one another, and the blood of Jesus, his Son, purifies us from all sin.
> —1 Jn 1:5-7 (1 Cor 6:19-20)

To be the "temple of God" means to be his dwelling place, or, as we have it expressed in Eph. 2:22, the "habitation of God." It is almost impossible for the heart of man to conceive of anything so amazing, but if we believe the Bible at all, we *must* believe that it is most blessedly true that our hearts are the home of our God, and that he does continually seek to find a dwelling place there.

> For the Lord has chosen Zion, / he has desired it for his dwelling: "This my resting place for ever and ever; / here I will sit enthroned, for I have desired it.—Ps 132:13-14

> Here I am! I stand at the door and knock. If anyone hears my voice and opens the door, I will come in and eat with him, and he with me.—Rv 3:20

Like the sunlight which fills the air all around us, and enters wherever there is an opening, so does the presence of God fill the whole universe around us, and enters every heart that opens to receive him.

> Jesus replied, "If anyone loves me, he will obey my teaching. My Father will love him, and we will come to him and make our home with him.—Jn 14:23 (1 Cor 7:1)

> Since we have these promises, dear friends, let us purify ourselves from everything that contaminates body and spirit, perfecting holiness out of reverence for God.—2 Cor 7:1

The Lord's dwelling place must be clean from "everything that contaminates body and spirit," in the very nature of things; and every soul that recognizes the blessed fact of his abiding presence will find itself stirred up to get rid of all that is contrary to his will.

> Sing, O Daughter of Zion; / shout aloud, O Israel! / Be glad and rejoice with all your heart, / O Daughter of Jerusalem! / The Lord has taken away your punishment, / he has turned back your enemy. / The Lord, the King of Israel, is with you; / never again will you fear any harm / On that day they will say to Jerusalem, / "Do not fear, O Zion; / do not let your hands hang limp. / The Lord your God is with you, / he is mighty to save. / He will take great delight in you, / he will quiet you with his love, / he will rejoice over you with singing."—Zp 3:14-17

How then shall we come into personal and practical recognition of this blessed fact that "the Lord encamps around us" and is in our midst?

A few extracts from a book called *The Practice of the Presence of God,* written by an old monk of the 17th century, will teach us the road to this glorious consummation.

We must establish ourselves in a sense of God's presence by a continual secret conversation with him, in freedom and simplicity. We must consider God as always with us, and as abiding in us; and must keep ourselves in His presence by a silent and secret conversation with him, thinking of him the oftenest we can. A little lifting up of the heart suffices; a little remembrance of Him, a single act of inward worship, even in the midst of business; these are the methods by which the heart comes to realize His abiding presence.

Let us think of Him, then, the most we can; let us accustom ourselves by degrees to this small but holy exercise. Nobody perceives it; and nothing is easier than to repeat often in the day these little internal adorations. This exercise consists in short ejaculations offered to God, as for instance, "O Lord, here I am, all devoted to thee," or "Lord, I thank thee that thou art present with me"; or, "Lord, make me what thou wouldst have me to be"; or any other form of words that love may suggest. We must do this without effort or constraint, recalling our minds to God mildly and with tranquillity, as often as we find we are wandering from him.

He requires no great matters of us: a little remembrance of Him from time to time, a little adoration: sometimes to pray for His grace, sometimes to offer Him your sufferings, and sometimes to return Him thanks for the favors He has given you and still gives you; reminding yourself of Him the oftenest you can. Lift up your heart to Him whenever you are reminded of Him, even at your meals, and when you are in company. You need not cry very loud, for He can hear the most secret whisper in your soul.

Use yourself by degrees to this little silent exercise, and you will at last form such a habit of recognizing His abiding presence, that you will never lose the consciousness of it."

All this means simply this, that we "acknowledge God" in all our ways by saying over each moment of our life, "The Lord is here"; and by doing *whatever* we do to his glory.

So whether you eat or drink or whatever you do, do it all for the glory of God.—1 Cor 10:31

How have I erred! God is my home
 And God himself is here;
Why have I looked so far for him
 Who is nowhere but near?

For God is never so far off
 As even to be near;
He is within; our spirit is
 The home he holds most dear.

To think of him as by our side,
 Is almost as untrue,
As to remove his throne beyond
 Those starry skies of blue.

So, all the while I thought myself
 Homeless, forlorn, and weary,
Missing my joy, I walked the earth
 Myself God's sanctuary.

SIXTEEN

The "I" Religion
and the "Not I" Religion

Foundation Text— *I have been crucified with Christ and I no longer live, but Christ lives in me. The life I live in the body, I live by faith in the Son of God, who loved me and gave himself for me.* —Gal 2:20

"I no longer live, but Christ lives in me." In all living there is one principal center around which the life revolved, and for the sake of which it acts. Generally this center is the "I" or self. Everything is calculated with reference to its influence on self; what gain or what improvement to one's personal standing or prospects will come from certain courses of action? How will it affect *me* ? These are the continual underlying questions. The Prodigal Son is an illustration of this.

> When he came to his senses, he said, "How many of my father's hired men have food to spare, and here I am starving to death! I will set out and go back to my father and say to him: Father, I have sinned against heaven and against you. I am no longer worthy to be called your son; make me like one of your hired men.
> —Lk 15:17-19

The son had no thought of the father's love or sorrow or longing; his only care was to get comfort and food for himself;

and his expectations could rise no higher than to be a servant in his father's household, where he would find "food to spare."

This is always the first selfish way of the human heart; we do not consider how our heavenly Father loves us, and longs for us, and grieves over our wandering, and will rejoice at our return; but we ask what *we* shall get by returning, what personal gain will accrue to *us*, how much better off *we* shall be for giving our allegiance to Christ. It is the "I" religion only, that we can comprehend at first.

> So he got up and went to his father.
> "But while he was still a long way off, his father saw him and was filled with compassion for him; he ran to his son, threw his arms around him and kissed him.
> The son said to him, "Father, I have sinned against heaven and against you. I am no longer worthy to be called your son."
> But the father said to his servants, "Quick! Bring the best robe and put it on him. Put a ring on his finger and sandals on his feet. Bring the fattened calf and kill it. Let's have a feast and celebrate. For this son of mine was dead and is alive again; he was lost and is found." So they began to celebrate.—Lk 15:20-24

In the father's embrace the "I" religion is swept away, and all thoughts of being a "hired man, with food to spare," vanish before the "best robe," and the "fattened calf," and the merry feast of welcome over "the son who was dead and is alive."

Sooner or later the child of God, if his spiritual life develops as it ought, comes to this place of insight, where thoughts of self vanish in the wondrous revelation of the Father's heart.

But the "I" religion is not lost all at once; nor is it confined only to the unenlightened sinner.

> Meanwhile, the older son was in the field. When he came near the house, he heard music and dancing. So he called one of the servants and asked him what was going on. "Your brother has come," he replied, "and your father has killed the fattened calf because he has him back safe and sound."
> The older brother became angry and refused to go in. So his father went out and pleaded with him. But he answered his father,

"Look! All these years I've been slaving for you and never disobeyed your orders. Yet you never gave me even a young goat so I could celebrate with my friends. But when this son of yours who has squandered your property with prostitutes comes home, you kill the fattened calf for him!"

"My son," the father said, "you are always with me, and everything I have is yours. But we had to celebrate and be glad, because this brother of yours was dead and is alive again; he was lost and is found."—Lk 15:25-32

The "elder brother," who lived at home with the father, and shared all his possessions, thought only of himself at this supreme moment of the father's joy, and had no sympathy with it. He felt himself to be badly used, and declared that his rights had not been recognized, nor his true merits appreciated. "Look, all these years I've been slaving for you, and yet you never did such things for me." Self was uppermost still in the heart of this son, who yet had been in one sense a good son, faithful in his father's service. But it was the "I" religion still. He could not forget himself.

There are some of God's children even now, who, like this "elder brother," in every emergency think of themselves first of all, and consider that their own rights and their own deserts ought always to have the first claim, both inwardly and outwardly.

"What do you want me to do for you?" he asked.

They replied, "Let one of us sit at your right and the other at your left in your glory." . . .

When the ten heard about this, they became indignant with James and John. Jesus called them together and said, "You know that those who are regarded as rulers of the Gentiles lord it over them, and their high officials exercise authority over them. Not so with you. Instead, whoever wants to become great among you must be your servant, and whoever wants to be first must be slave of all. For even the Son of Man did not come to be served, but to serve, and to give his life as a ransom for many.

—Mk 10:36-37, 41-45

James and John were thinking of themselves. They wanted the highest places, and to be chief among their brethren, and they sought it by the way of the "I" religion. "Let one of us sit at your right and the other at your left in your glory." Place, power, position, honor, glory, these are the considerations that move the soul in whom the "I" religion reigns. And such souls cannot even see that the only true honor and glory are to be found in the "not I" religion, where we become the greatest by being the servant of all.

Nobody should seek his own good, but the good of others.
—1 Cor 10:24

Do nothing out of selfish ambition or vain conceit, but in humility consider others better than yourselves. Each of you should look not only to your own interests, but also to the interests of others.
Your attitude should be the same as that of Christ Jesus: / Who, being in very nature God, / did not consider equality with God something to be grasped, / but made himself nothing, / taking the very nature of a servant, / being made in human likeness. / And being found in appearance as a man, / he humbled himself / and became obedient to death—even death on a cross!
—Phil 2:3-8

Paul knew both of these religions. While he was a Pharisee, he had been full of the "I" religion, and had made a great show in it. But when his eyes were opened to see the beauty of the "not I" religion, he counted all the other rubbish in comparison with it.

Though I myself have reasons for such confidence.
If anyone else thinks he has reasons to put confidence in the flesh, I have more: circumcised on the eighth day, of the people of Israel, of the tribe of Benjamin, a Hebrew of Hebrews; in regard to the law, a Pharisee; as for zeal, persecuting the church; as for legalistic righteousness, faultless.
But whatever was to my profit I now consider loss for the sake of Christ. What is more, I consider everything a loss compared to the surpassing greatness of knowing Christ Jesus my Lord, for

whose sake I have lost all things. I consider them rubbish, that I may gain Christ and be found in him, not having a righteousness of my own that comes from the law, but that which is through faith in Christ—the righteousness that comes from God and is by faith.—Phil 3:4-9

All that Paul had to say for himself, all that fine system of self-righteousness, all that "confidence in the flesh," that earnest "zeal," that blameless "righteousness" of which he had been so justly proud, all in his "I" religion, vanished into thin air at the sight of Christ, and the excellency that was in him. Paul's big "I," which before had filled his whole horizon, wilted down into nothing before the revelation of God in the face of Jesus Christ. "I no longer live," he cried, "but Christ lives in me." He had learned the lesson of the "not I" religion.

My ears had heard of you / but now my eyes have seen you. / Therefore I despise myself / and repent in dust and ashes.
—Job 42:5-6

The book of Job is the story of the "I" religion, and the process of its change into the "not I" religion. Job was a good man at first, but not at first a spiritual man.

In the land of Uz there lived a man whose name was Job. This man was blameless and upright; he feared God and shunned evil. . . .
Then the Lord said to Satan, "Have you considered my servant Job? There is no one on earth like him; he is blameless and upright, a man who fears God and shuns evil."—Job 1:1, 8

Even God pronounced him to be "blameless and upright." And yet Job was full of himself, his own goodness, his own honor, his own benevolence, his own reputation. Read for instance the twenty-ninth chapter and count the personal pronouns used there, and you will see that they are used fifty times. It is all *I, me, my,* from beginning to end; while God is referred to only three times.

And is not this chapter a simple transcript of many chapters in the lives of some of God's most faithful servants, whose greatest delight is to dwell upon their own good deeds, or their own valuable possessions, and to recount them to others? Have we any such chapters in the unwritten books of our autobiographies, dear readers? It may help us if we will mark a line with ink underneath each *I, me* and *my* of this chapter in Job as a reminder of our similar chapters.

Contrast with these utterances of Job the words of David in the Psalms. Notice for instance Psalm 118.

Here the Lord is mentioned, with the pronouns *he, his, him* and *you,* forty-six times: and all that is said concerning *I, me* and *my,* is simply to set forth my need and my distress, and to show how the Lord helped and delivered. In the twenty-nine verses of this Psalm, all but four tell of something good or great that the Lord does.

> I will exalt you, my God the King; / I will praise your name for ever and ever. / Every day I will praise you / and extol your name for ever and ever. / Great is the Lord and most worthy of praise; / his greatness no one can fathom. / One generation will commend your works to another; / they will tell of your mighty acts. / They will speak of the glorious splendor of your majesty, / and I will meditate on your wonderful works. / They will tell of the power of your awesome works, / and I will proclaim your great deeds. / They will celebrate your abundant goodness / and joyfully sing of your righteousness.—Ps 145:1-7 (Ps 105:1-2)

People are far more ready to "celebrate" the memory of their own abundant goodness than of God's. The book of Job is full of what I am. The book of Psalms is full of what God is.

Job expressed the feelings of a man who had great possessions. The Psalms express the feelings of a man who possessed nothing but the living God.

Contrast Job 1:3 with Psalm 73:25-26.

> And he owned seven thousand sheep, three thousand camels, five hundred yoke of oxen and five hundred donkeys, and had a large number of servants. He was the greatest man among all the people of the East.—Job 1:3

Whom have I in heaven but you? / And being with you, I desire nothing on earth. / My flesh and my heart may fail, / but God is the strength of my heart / and my portion forever. —Ps 73:25-26

Lord, you have assigned me my portion and my cup; / you have made my lot secure. / The boundary lines have fallen for me in pleasant places; / surely I have a delightful inheritance.

—Ps 16:5-6

To have the Lord for our portion is an "inheritance" far better than any of the great possessions of earth, and confers upon the soul infinitely greater honor.

The "I" religion justifies itself. The "not I" religion justifies God. Contrast Job 32:1-2 with Psalm 96.

So these three men stopped answering Job, because he was righteous in his own eyes. But Elihu son of Barakel the Buzite, of the family of Ram, became very angry with Job for justifying himself rather than God. —Job 32:1-2

Sing to the Lord a new song; / sing to the Lord, all the earth. / Sing to the Lord, praise his name; / proclaim his salvation day after day. / Declare his glory among the nations, / his marvelous deeds among all peoples. / For great is the Lord and most worthy of praise; / he is to be feared above all gods. / For all the gods of the nations are idols, / but the Lord made the heavens. / Splendor and majesty are before him; / strength and glory are in his sanctuary. / Ascribe to the Lord, O families of nations, / ascribe to the Lord glory and strength. / Ascribe to the Lord the glory due his name; / bring an offering and come into his courts.

—Ps 96:1-8

Job was full of himself. The writer of the Psalms was full of the Lord. "Of thee, oh Lord, will I sing," is the language of the "not I" religion. "Of me, oh myself, will I sing," is the language of the "I" religion.

Job had to suffer the loss of all things, and out of this loss have a revelation of God, before he could get rid of the "I" religion.

The Lord said to Job: "Will the one who contends with the Almighty correct him?

Let him who accuses God answer him!"
Then Job answered the Lord;
"I am unworthy—how can I reply to you? / I put my hand over my mouth. / I spoke once, but I have no answer— / twice, but I will say no more." / Then the Lord spoke to Job out of the storm:
—Job 40:1-6

Then Job replied to the Lord: "I know that you can do all things; / no plan of yours can be thwarted. / You asked, 'Who is this that obscures my counsel without knowledge?' / Surely I spoke of things I did not understand, / things too wonderful for me to know. / You said, 'Listen now, and I will speak; / I will question you, / and you shall answer me.' / My ears had heard of you / but now my eyes have seen you. / Therefore I despise myself / and repent in dust and ashes."—Job 42:1-6

God took away all his possessions, everything in which he delighted, or upon which he could rest; and then "out of the storm" he answered Job with a revelation of himself.

And just so is it sometimes now in the lives of God's children who have great possessions, whether inward or outward. Only "out of the storm" that has destroyed their possessions, can they have a revelation of God.

"All these I have kept," the young man said. "What do I still lack?"
Jesus answered, "If you want to be perfect, go, sell your possessions and give to the poor, and you will have treasure in heaven. Then come, follow me."
When the young man heard this, he went away sad, because he had great wealth.
Then Jesus said to his disciples, "I tell you the truth, it is hard for a rich man to enter the kingdom of heaven. Again I tell you, it is easier for a camel to go through the eye of a needle than for a rich man to enter the kingdom of God."—Mt 19:20-24

To enter into the "kingdom of heaven," all dependence upon earthly riches, whether of money, or of reputation, or of good deeds, must be given up. The "poor in spirit" alone can enter here. "To gain the whole world," in any sense, however subtle, is to lose one's soul in the same subtle sense.

> Then he called the crowd to him along with his disciples and said: "If anyone would come after me, he must deny himself and take up his cross and follow me. For whoever wants to save his life will lose it, but whoever loses his life for me and for the gospel will save it. What good is it for a man to gain the whole world, yet forfeit his soul? Or what can a man give in exchange for his soul?—Mk 8:34-37

There are some of God's own children who make great outward gains in things that minister to self, even in their religious lives; who have wonderful religious experiences, and do great religious works, and receive honor from all men; but who yet, in this gaining, have so degraded their finest impulses, and deadened their spiritual life, as to bury their souls under a mountain of selfhood, until they have to all intents and purposes "lost their life."

> Then Jesus said to his disciples, "If anyone would come after me, he must deny himself and take up his cross and follow me. For whoever wants to save his life will lose it, but whoever loses his life for me will find it. What good will it be for a man if he gains the whole world, yet forfeits his soul? Or what can a man give in exchange for his soul?"—Mt 16:24-26 (Lk 9:23-25)

The "not I" religion is the religion that denies self, that says to this "I," "I am a stranger to you and do not wish to have anything to do with you." It denies self, not in the sense of making self miserable, of setting self on a pinnacle and sticking prongs into it to hurt it; but in the sense of utterly refusing to recognize its claims or even its existence, and of enthroning the Christ-life in its stead always and everywhere.

To "take up the cross" does not mean to make this "I" miserable, as is too often thought. It means to put this "I" to death, to crucify it; not to make it suffer but to kill it outright.

It means to lose our own self-life truly and literally, and to have the divine life, the life hid with Christ in God, to reign in its stead.

> We were therefore buried with him through baptism into death in order that, just as Christ was raised from the dead through the glory of the Father, we too may live a new life. . . .
> In the same way, count yourselves dead to sin but alive to God in Christ Jesus.—Rom 6:4, 11

The only way out of the "I" religion into the "not I" religion is by the death of self. We must die that we may live.

We must cease to be alive to self, and must consent to be alive only to God. And this means practically that we literally are not to care how self is treated, nor what self gains, nor what becomes of self, but only how God is treated, and what brings gain and joy to him. The trouble with all our religion is its tendency to selfishness. Its first and foremost thought is always for self; and this cannot but taint the whole character. if it is right to think of self first in the most sacred of all things, it cannot be wrong to think of self first in all minor things. We are continually seeking to save ourselves and to please ourselves.

> Those who passed by hurled insults at him, shaking their heads and saying, "So! You who are going to destroy the temple and build it in three days, come down from the cross and save yourself!"
> In the same way the chief priests and the teachers of the law mocked him among themselves. "He saved others," they said, "but he can't save himself!—Mk 15:29-31
>
> We who are strong ought to bear with the failings of the weak and not to please ourselves. Each of us should please his neighbor for his good, to build him up. For even Christ did not please himself but, as it is written: "The insults of those who insult you have fallen on me."—Rom 15:1-3

Christ "saved others, but he cannot save himself." Christ "did not please himself." And if we are living the Christ-life we shall know that we also are "not to please ourselves," nor to save ourselves, but are to save and to please others.

> Carry each other's burdens, and in this way you will fulfill the law of Christ.—Gal 6:2

Alas! how far we are from this Christ-like burden bearing. Our own burdens fill the whole horizon for us, and we can scarcely see, much less carry, the burdens of others. Indeed we often feel that, if everyone had their rights, *our* burdens and *our* needs would be recognized by all around us as being of paramount importance to all other things.

We will move heaven and earth in our efforts to save ourselves, and we will scarcely lift a finger to try to save or to please others. And this selfishness of our "I" religion taints our views of God. We are so selfish ourselves, that we are unable to give one single generous or unselfish attribute to him, and we think he must be all the time looking out for his rights and his glory, just as we are for ours. We are actually afraid to trust him to save us, because we know our own selfish unwillingness to save others. We think he is "altogether like us." This is the "I" religion.

> You use your mouth for evil / and harness your tongue to deceit. / You speak continually against your brother / and slander your own mother's son. / These things you have done and I kept silent; / you thought I was altogether like you. / But I will rebuke you / and accuse you to your face.—Ps 50:19-21

Even Christians "speak continually," not of God's great goodness, but of their brother's great failures, and try to exalt themselves at their brother's expense. And naturally they transfer the same selfish characteristics to God, and think he also is entirely absorbed in the advancement of his own glory, no matter at whose expense it may have to be.

But the "not I" religion is just the opposite. It has handed self over bodily to death, and has ceased to be interested in it. It has forgotten self in its absorption in God. It expects nothing from self, but everything from God; and it demands nothing for self, but seeks to lavish all on the Lord.

> When a woman who had lived a sinful life in that town learned that Jesus was eating at the Pharisee's house, she brought an alabaster jar of perfume, and as she stood behind him at his feet weeping, she began to wet his feet with her tears. Then she wiped them with her hair, kissed them and poured perfume on them. . . . Then he turned toward the woman and said to Simon, "Do you see this woman? I came into your house. You did not give me any water for my feet, but she wet my feet with her tears and wiped them with her hair. You did not give me a kiss, but this woman, from the time I entered, has not stopped kissing my feet. You did not put oil on my head, but she has poured perfume on my feet. Therefore, I tell you, her many sins have been forgiven—for she loved much. But he who has been forgiven little loves little.—Lk 7:37-38, 44-48

The "not I" religion pours out its most precious gifts as a love offering upon its Lord, and asks for no return; but it receives most abundant and unexpected measure. This poor woman "who had lived a sinful life" never dreamed that she deserved anything, but she found herself overwhelmed with blessing.

> To some who were confident of their own righteousness and looked down on everybody else, Jesus told this parable: "Two men went up to the temple to pray, one a Pharisee and the other a tax collector. The Pharisee stood up and prayed about himself: 'God, I thank you that I am not like all other men—robbers, evil-doers, adulterers—or even like this tax collector. I fast twice a week and give a tenth of all I get.'
> "But the tax collector stood at a distance. He would not even look up to heaven, but beat his breast and said, 'God, have mercy on me, a sinner.'
> I tell you that this man, rather than the other, went home justified before God. For everyone who exalts himself will be humbled, and he who humbles himself will be exalted."
> —Lk 18:9-14

This Pharisee had the "I" religion. "I thank you that I am not like all other men." The tax collector had nothing to say for himself, but that he was a needy sinner.

Some of the most religious people of the day are the greatest Pharisees; they have the most of the "I" religion. "I am right," they say, "and you, if you differ from me, are wrong. I ought to be put foremost, for I know best. I am the one to have place and authority, for I am the best fitted to assume it. My rights must be considered, for they are the most important." The "I" religion compels everything to come up to its own standard. The "not I" religion covers all things with a mantle of Christ-like love; it is patient and kind"; it "does not envy"; "it does not boast and is not proud"; it "is not self-seeking, and is not easily angered, it keeps no record of wrongs"; "it always protects, always trusts, always hopes, always perseveres."

Such a person walks as Christ walked.

Whoever claims to live in him must walk as Jesus did.—1 Jn 2:6

For it is commendable if a man bears up under the pain of unjust suffering because he is conscious of God. But how is it to your credit if you receive a beating for doing wrong and endure it? But if you suffer for doing good and you endure it, this is commendable before God. To this you were called, because Christ suffered for you, leaving you an example, that you should follow in his steps. / "He committed no sin, / and no deceit was found in his mouth." / When they hurled their insults at him, he did not retaliate; when he suffered, he made no threats. Instead, he entrusted himself to him who judges justly.—1 Pt 2:19-23

The "not I" religion bears injustice, and misunderstanding, and lack of appreciation, and revilings, and snubbings, and being spoken against, and having its name cast out as evil, with patience, and even often with joy.

Looking at his disciples, he said: / "Blessed are you who are poor, / for yours is the kingdom of God. / Blessed are you who hunger now, / for you will be satisfied. / Blessed are you who weep now, / for you will laugh. / Blessed are you when men hate you, / when they exclude you and insult you / and reject your name as evil, because of the Son of Man. / "Rejoice in that day and leap for joy, because great is your reward in heaven. For that is how their fathers treated the prophets. / "But woe to you who are rich, / for you have already received your comfort. / Woe to you who are well fed now, / for you will go hungry. / Woe to you who laugh now, / for you will mourn and weep. / Woe to you when all men speak well of you, / for that is how their fathers treated the false prophets.

"But I tell you who hear me: Love your enemies, do good to those who hate you, bless those who curse you, pray for those who mistreat you. If someone strikes you on one cheek, turn to him the other also. If someone takes your cloak, do not stop him from taking your tunic. Give to everyone who asks you, and if anyone takes what belongs to you, do not demand it back. Do to others as you would have them do to you.

"If you love those who love you, what credit is that to you? Even 'sinners' love those who love them. And if you do good to those who are good to you, what credit is that to you? Even 'sinners' do that. And if you lend to those from whom you expect repayment, what credit is that to you? Even 'sinners' lend to 'sinners,' expecting to be repaid in full. But love your enemies, do good to them, and lend to them without expecting to get anything back. Then your reward will be great, and you will be sons of the Most High, because he is kind to the ungrateful and wicked. Be merciful, just as your Father is merciful.—Lk 6:20-36

If the Christ-life is the reigning life in us, we shall do the works of Christ. If the self-life is the reigning life, we will do the works of self.

Which sort of works is it that we do?

There is therefore now no condemnation for those who are in Christ Jesus. For the law of the Spirit of life in Christ Jesus has set me free from the law of sin and death. For God has done what the law, weakened by the flesh, could not do: sending his own Son in the likeness of sinful flesh and for sin, he condemned sin in the flesh, in order that the just requirement of the law might be fulfilled in us, who walk not according to the flesh but according to the Spirit. For those who live according to the flesh set their minds on the things of the flesh, but those who live according to the Spirit set their minds on the things of the Spirit.

—Rom 8:1-5 RSV

The "I" religion is the religion of the flesh. The "not I" religion is the religion of the Spirit.

It is very possible to "walk according to the flesh," even in a religious life. If we are seeking for the highest places or the greatest honor in our church work or service, if we are standing up for our rights, if we are on the watch for affronts, and are keen to resent them, if we consider everything in its relation to ourselves, if we look out for our own interests first, if we provoke one another and envy one another; then, no matter how great may be our reputation for piety, we have never got beyond the "I" religion, and are in truth "walking according to the flesh."

> The entire law is summed up in a single command: "Love your neighbor as yourself." If you keep on biting and devouring each other, watch out or you will be destroyed by each other.
>
> So I say, live by the Spirit, and you will not gratify the desires of the sinful nature. For the sinful nature desires what is contrary to the Spirit, and the Spirit what is contrary to the sinful nature. They are in conflict with each other, so that you do not do what you want. But if you are led by the Spirit, you are not under law.
>
> The acts of the sinful nature are obvious: sexual immorality, impurity and debauchery; idolatry and witchcraft; hatred, discord, jealousy, fits of rage, selfish ambition, dissensions, factions and envy; drunkenness, orgies, and the like. I warn you, as I did before, that those who live like this will not inherit the kingdom of God.
>
> But the fruit of the Spirit is love, joy, peace, patience, kindness, goodness, faithfulness, gentleness and self-control. Against such things there is no law. Those who belong to Christ Jesus have crucified the sinful nature with its passions and desires. Since we live by the Spirit, let us keep in step with the Spirit. Let us not become conceited, provoking and envying each other.
>
> —Gal 5:14-26

To sum up the whole matter then, the choice is continually before us as to which form of religion ours shall be. Shall it be I who live, or not I? Shall it be self or Christ?

This question confronts us at every moment of our living, and must be answered continually, either consciously or unconsciously. In each event that meets us, self clamors for recognition, and at each clamor it may be crucified and its claims ignored. Always and everywhere we may put off the old self of the "I" religion, and may put on the new self of the "not I" religion.

> You were taught, with regard to your former way of life, to put off your old self, which is being corrupted by its deceitful desires; to be made new in the attitude of your minds; and to put on the new self, created to be like God in true righteousness and holiness.
> —Eph 4:22-24

In all Christian experience there is a progress from the "I" religion to the "not I" religion. At first with all of us it is I and not Christ at all; then it becomes I *and* Christ; then it becomes Christ first and only a little of I. But has it come yet with any of us, as it had to Paul when he wrote the verse which is the foundation of our lesson, to be Christ only and not I at all?